DATE DUE

GAYLORD   PRINTED IN U.S.A.

The Land and People of Greece

PORTRAITS OF THE NATIONS SERIES

The Land and People of

GREECE

By

THEODORE GIANAKOULIS

Illustrated from Photographs

J. B. LIPPINCOTT COMPANY : PHILADELPHIA & NEW YORK

Contents

*The illustrations, from photographs, are grouped
in a signature following page 54*

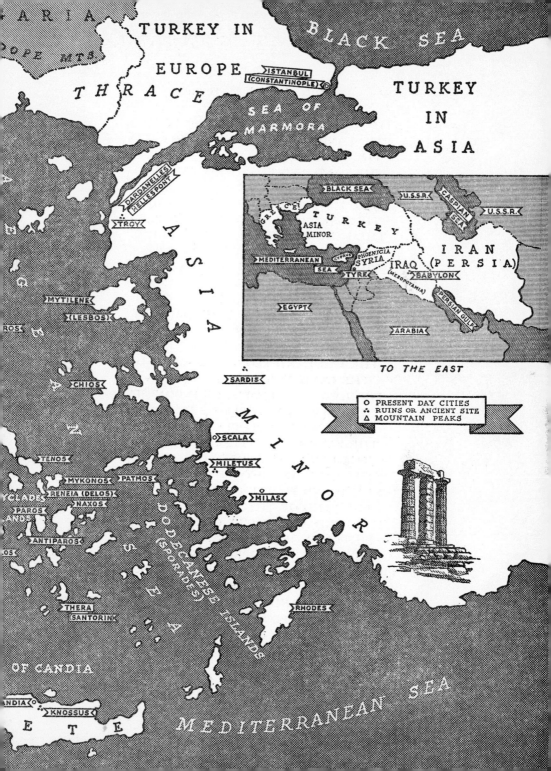

The Land and People of Greece

Chapter One

THE MARBLE HAND
(The Mainland of Greece)

REACHING down from Europe, the Greek peninsula is not unlike a wrist and open hand with part of a long cuff or sleeve at the top. Southward, Eubœa, Attica, and the promontories of Peloponnesus roughly suggest spread-out fingers touching the sea. Beyond and around them are hundreds and hundreds of little islands. And behind Peloponnesus the sea makes a deep indentation, the Gulf of Corinth, almost severing the fingers from the palm. The sea runs up everywhere into Greece and has always been an important part of Greek life and destiny.

When you see the Greek landscape you are not aware of big plains, lofty mountains, towering cities. There are no important-looking estates, or great railroad lines threading cities and towns. The general impression is of hemmed-in, V-shaped valleys, small plains, compartments and terraces, broken up by a continuous interlacing of mountains and sea, all basking in gentle, golden sunlight. Three-quarters of the whole area, (about 50,000 square miles) is covered by rugged and jumbled mountains that never rise to a high mass of ranges but seem like petrified billows. There is a legend that when God had created the world, He went from country to country to adorn it with rocks of all sizes, shapes and colors kept in a huge sack, and as He came back over Greece, the sack suddenly tore open and all the small bits that were left tumbled down.

Mount Olympus, the highest peak, is the only one nearing the 10,000-foot mark. Mount Parnassus, in central Greece, and Mount

Taygetus, near the southern extremity of Peloponnesus, are each about 8,000 feet high.

The main Pindus Ranges fill the Greek mainland from end to end. They stand out like a backbone. Parallel to the Aegean Sea on the northeast, out into it to the east, parallel with the Adriatic and Ionian Seas on the west, out or parallel, everywhere the Pindus folds run north to south, detailing into a tangle of smaller peaks and ranges gashed by the Gulf of Corinth, and reappear as the numerous rugged islands dotting the eastern Mediterranean.

One would expect to find Greece, with so many mountains, rich in metals, minerals or coal. But the mountains of Greece, with many surface scars, caverns, sink holes and subterranean channels, are poor in these resources. They do contain some lignite, lead, iron, and chrome, but not nearly enough to feed large industries or to export. However, to a great extent, the mountains are composed of a beautiful marble. It is the main building stone of the people. It has been so for many centuries. And how well the Greek people have learned to work with it! Their whole civilization is built in marble. The ancients built their temples and made their monuments and statues of marble, as did the later Byzantines. The people today use it for churches, hospitals, and large schools. Milk-white or glittering translucent, pink or creamy marble, so fine and delicate that thin panes of it as church windows let through the diffused light of Greece.

One sees everywhere in Greece the marble cutters at work. With hammers, chisels, levers and rulers in hands, they move like dark shadows on the white background, measuring and cutting the white blocks or shaping a column, a cornice, a tombstone.

More than by mountains, Greek civilization has been influenced by the sea. The Mediterranean, which bounds Greece on the east, south and west, is the largest sea in the world. From Gibraltar to the Suez Canal, there is a wide lapis blue stretch of well over two thousand miles. The "big sea" pushes all around, touching the shores and the lands of many sovereign states. To the east of the Greek mainland it forms the "wine-dark" Aegean, lying between Greece and Asia Minor, and guarding the northeast approaches to the Dardanelles. On the west it forms the Ionian Sea, between Greece and Italy, and between Crete, the Cyclades Islands and Peloponnesus it makes another sea roughly one hundred miles wide.

The subtropical air of the sea penetrates sheltered valleys, canals and straits, and circulates into the hills and back country, determining the color of the Greek sky and landscape, even the temperament and ideals of the people. Along the coasts it has created a narrow strip of pleasant and fertile land, green with vineyards and olive groves.

The mainland consists of various long established districts. In the north, from west to east, are Epirus, Macedonia and Thrace, bounded by Albania, Yugoslavia, Bulgaria and Turkey. Epirus is small and rocky, Thrace confined by hills, but Macedonia is large, and open and green. Mount Olympus stands on the boundary between Macedonia and the storied land of Thessaly to the south.

Central Greece includes Bœotia, with its ancient city of Thebes, and Phocis, where the oracle of Delphi, perched high on the slopes of Parnassus, looks down to the far Gulf of Corinth and on across to the "bright isle of Pelops." Attica is separated from Bœotia by a chain of mountains, and near Athens are the peaks of Mount Pentelicus, famous for its gold-tinged marble, and Hymettus, equally famous for its golden honey.

The only land boundary of Greece is on the north. It extends east-west for nearly five hundred miles, along the Rhodope Massif and the Grammos-Vitsi Ranges. They separate Greece from her Balkan neighbors. It was through these mountains that the first Asiatic nomads came at the beginning of the Bronze Age (3,000-2,600 B.C.), and the Indo-Europeans about 2,000 B.C. and again from 1,200 to 1,000 B.C. Other nomads had to cross over the numerous Aegean islands or over the steppes of the Ural-Caspian Gap, and through the Hellespont.

The North is green in summer and white in winter. Cold winds sweep in from the Asiatic high-pressure area. They blanket the mountains with snow, which piles up high and lasts long after the snow in the South has melted. Then, though the growing season is shorter, the soil is rich, well watered, and the crops more abundant. Everywhere there is greenness, from terraced hillsides to willow-draped riverbanks. The North is fenced with almost impassable mountains. But on the northeast, between mountains and sea, is the wide plain of Macedonia, the richest of Greece's lands. A big north-to-south depression, the Vardar Valley pass, separates the Pindus folds to the west from the Rhodope Massif to the northeast. It starts in the Hungarian plains, runs south through the Yugoslav Morava Valley (agricultural center of old Serbia), and opens up into the Salonika plains. This is the main artery, the shortest and most convenient route in and out. All land approaches lead into the Salonika plains. The important Athens-Salonika-Nice railway follows this route to the Yugoslav border, and connects with the Orient Express, linking northeastern Europe and the Middle East to the Persian Gulf. Farther east is a smaller depression, the Struma River pass, leading into Greece from Bulgaria. Still farther spreads the big plain of Thrace. Southeast of this plain, across the Aegean and actually in Turkey, there is a famous waterway about 50 miles long and 4 miles wide, uniting the Sea of Marmora with the Aegean. This is the Hellespont or Straits of Dardanelles, which is of great importance to all world powers, because in wartime the Straits can be made almost impregnable.

The magnet of northern Greece is the city of Salonika. Ancient and cosmopolitan, it is the second largest and most important Greek city (considering as the largest Athens and its port, the Piræus, together). Salonika is the terminus of four railways, and the seaport of southeastern Europe. It was always the military and commercial station on the main line of communication between the two continents. Everywhere about the city are monuments left through centuries by many invaders, who sacked or conquered and held the magnificent city for a while. Most remarkable among all the ancient and medieval monuments are the Byzantine churches of St. Sophia, St. George, and St. Demetrios, patron Saint of the town.

East and west of Salonika, the country is cut by many rivers.

Lively brooks feeding irrigation ditches crisscross the land. The rivers originate in northern hill cups and mountain plateaus. When the spring sun warms the earth and the thaws begin, they are rushing torrents and inundate the plains, hampering traffic and forming swamps that are hotbeds of malaria. But they make a rich flat soil, most productive in tobacco and grain. In the hills, oak, walnut and chestnut forests shelter picturesque little hamlets. Mountain meadows, carpeted with velvet grass, are the summer pastures for large flocks of goats, sheep or pigs.

Along the coastal area between sea and mountains, cities and towns are busy the year round, people coming and going over ancient earth roads and over a great modern highway still raw on the landscape. Near Salonika, a flourishing farm of three hundred acres and forty buildings, part of the American Farm School, founded by the late Dr. J. H. House to teach Greek boys American Agricultural methods, has survived wars and civil conflicts since its founding in 1902. Thousands are among its graduates, poor and rich, tobacco planters and members of the Agricultural Bank of Greece, the Ministry of Agriculture and other agencies.

In Macedonia the sun shines on giant American bulldozers and swift-moving tractors. Back and forth, up and down the miles of plains, around hills and through valleys, they are shifting soil, constructing levees, canals, dikes, opening strips for airport runways, draining estuaries and mud pools, cutting irrigation ditches. Reclamation of the Vardar River marshes alone in 1933, at a cost of 26 million dollars, added 325,000 acres of cultivatable land and provided settlement areas for 30,000 families of Greek refugees from Anatolia. Today these people are skilled farmers. Seventy million cubic yards of earth were moved to drain five hundred square miles in the Salonika plains alone. American dredgers and bulldozers have done more for this region than all the centuries of invading armies. For one thing, they have routed that ancient and deadly enemy, the malaria mosquito.

The second most important agricultural area is the five-thousand-square-mile plain of Thessaly, separated from the Salonika plains by the Cambunian Mountains. This area is divided almost equally by a range of low mountains, and is drained by the river Peneus, which rends through the mountains the steep canyon or Vale of Tempe, and rushes into the Gulf of Salonika.

Farther down, is the narrow gash which cuts the whole nation in two—the Gulf of Corinth. A four-mile-long, arrow-straight canal at the eastern end of the Gulf unites the Adriatic with the Aegean, and shortens the journey by two hundred miles. Twenty-six feet of water make it available for most steamers plying from Piræus to Marseilles or from Patras to Istanbul. Before the canal was cut in the late nineteenth century, boats were dragged across over a track, instead of making the stormy voyage around Cape Matapan, at the southern tip of Peloponnesus. At one place, parallel to the canal, traces of ancient walls can still be seen. They are the remains of the sacred enclosure of the famous fortified sanctuary of Poseidon, where the Isthmian Games were celebrated.

Southern Greece looks dry and dusty. The very towns and hamlets drowsing in the sun are almost indistinguishable from the landscape, except for the red-roofed and lime-coated houses of the shores, the windmills of the islands, and the dark clusters of cypresses shading silver-domed churches. Not even the thin scrub-pine forests or the hillslope patches and terraces, have the same lush green of those of the North. The shore line and the islands are almost one with the color of sea and yellowing fields. The rivers are short, barely trickling in the summer when needed most: rushing and torrential in winter. In summer, water is a major problem. Along the seacoast areas, wells are the only source of drinking water. It is lukewarm and brackish. The atmosphere is crystal clear: the air always dry: the temperature mild and pleasant, ranging from 40 to 60 degrees in winter, and 70 to 90 in summer, but the summer heat constantly tempered by sea or mountain breezes.

The South has two seasons, the wet and the dry. Most of the rainfall occurs in winter. But there are no monsoon rains, or leaden skies with water dripping for days or weeks. The rains here come like thundershowers, and pass away, leaving star-filled skies at night. For Greece is subject to both warm Mediterranean and cold Balkan winds, blowing at times in sudden and rapid succession, counterchecking one another. There is hardly any rain all summer. The earth is bone dry; the sun hot; the sky deep, deep blue. A bucketful or a trickle of water from a nearby dry river finds its way to the yellowing greenery of garden and field. The only true greenness the country presents is in the areas of clay lowlands where irrigation is practised. Here the crop yields are excellent, but these areas are few and far apart.

The brightest spot in the map of Greece is in the middle. This is the plain of Attica, in southeast central Greece. It is not large—about 1,000 square miles—and it is not over-fertile. But for its importance in history and culture, it is the heart of Greece. Here, on the southern side of the plain rises Athens, the white city of light, which was a beacon in the story of civilization, and where the centuries jostle one another in the streets. A little beyond lies the Saronic Gulf, scalloped with white beaches and lively summer resorts. The most famous spot is Loutraki, with warm springs, numerous hotels, bars, restaurants run by American-Greeks, and a casino. This is known as Greece's Coney Island.

On the Saronic Gulf is the great port of Piræus, the main artery of all sea traffic of the entire country. For its size the harbor is as busy as the port of New York, with all kinds of modern craft, gunboats native and foreign, rusty old tramps, sampans, cargo boats, steamers packed with tourists or pilgrims for the nearby islands, tiny Greek boats with imposing names, graceful yachts, small, long and narrow felluccas, and basket-masted American warships going or coming. Athens and its port have grown into one cosmopolitan city, linked by an electric railway, much as New York City is linked with Brooklyn.

Bustling with activity as never before in its long history, Athens, the capital, is the political and cultural center of Greece. A million and a half people live there. The whole world meets in its streets. Constitution Square, half open-air café, half park, is the civic center, the hub of Athenian life. Rows upon rows of little tables line the square, shaded by orange trees, oleanders and palms. And every seat is occupied by a potential politician! For now, as of old, every Athenian is in politics. Even the chance vendor or shoeshine boy winding among the little tables has his own idea as to how the government should be run and the world made a better place to live in! Greece is still very much a land of free-thinking and free-speaking people.

In the "violet-crowned" city are countless points of historic and artistic interest. The main artery is University Street. Here, in white marble buildings, are the University of Athens, the Academy and the Library.

North and south, over the half-hidden ancient stone roads, remains of ancient towns, some of whose names have long since been changed or forgotten, rise at every few miles of the road. Colossal blocks and fallen columns gleam among the olive trees, cypresses and grapevines. The fields are splattered with red poppies and white anemones. "Athena's owls" perched on ancient trees, peer out over the ruins.

Seen from aloft, Greece is so beautiful, with its vivid blues and molten gold and the breathtaking forms of its mountains. But, actually the burnt earth is a tissue of scars. For Greece is one of the most ancient continuously inhabited parts of the world and all too plainly shows the ruins of forgotten and all-too-well remembered wars and the destruction of national resources caused by man's greed, stupidity and neglect. The forests are gone; the rivers shrunken from erosion.

Everywhere, too, one sees the tireless struggle to wrest a living from the impoverished earth. For centuries the people have toiled to grow enough grain for themselves, never with complete success. The land is worked over and over, the whole surface is one big patchwork of colors: dark tobacco fields, green strips of maize and barley, terraces of steep vineyards, gray squares of olive groves. In sheltered places there are occasional clusters of black cypresses where a church or monastery has been wrought into or out of sheer granite by the patient hands of men of faith.

Countless narrow earth and stone roads, half-hidden and worn smooth by generations of people, cut through the hills, wind around the valleys, far into the back country and to the remote plateaus. One feels the timelessness and the mellowness of the Greek world. One senses a people close to the earth and the basic realities of existence.

On the other hand, there is an all-inclusive network of modern hard-paved roads running the length and breadth of the land. It circles the Peloponnesus; runs through Athens, crosses Thessaly picking up confluent roads from the west, and ends at Salonika.

This highway is typical of the changes which have come over Greece since the last war. Many projects of land reclamation, industrial development and education have accelerated the tempo of activity. Already there is less poverty and more opportunity. The immediate future is bright and filled with promise, for with increasing economic security and increasing production there will follow new expressions— in social and political changes, in science and in art—of the ancient Greek ideals.

Chapter Two

THE PEARLS OF THE AEGEAN

(The Islands)

A FIRST sight of the "pearls of the Aegean" is an unforgettable experience. No other islands in the world are so storied, and no sea so rich in history, in culture and in legend. "Anyone who has not seen the islands, has not really seen Greece" is a saying. Passing by boat from Greece to Asia Minor, one is always in sight of innumerable islands of all sizes, shapes and colors—each having its special character and charm. A few are good sized and through many centuries acted as stepping-stones and places of barter; they are now stops on the island-hopping air routes over the Mediterranean. But most of the Aegean isles are tiny dots on the sea, protected by their remoteness and unimportance, idyllic little worlds of beauty and peace.

The long Mediterranean is Europe's highway by sea. In ancient times it was the center of the world's gravity. After the discovery of the new continent to the west, and a new route to the Orient, the big sea lost its importance as the main thoroughfare. Civilization's center of gravity then shifted to the Atlantic.

The isles of Greece were the scene of one of the earliest societies. Centuries before the advent of Christianity, legends of gods and men were born here and deeds enacted that went down into the cultural heritage of the Western world. Law, navigation, trade and democracy in its first primitive forms had their origins here. Aegean trading methods, customs and art forms moved from island to island.

The sprinkled isles of the Aegean, Browning's "lily on lily," almost overlace one another, their white beaches and gentle climate inviting the voyager to linger. Dazzling little towns pop out of a pastoral landscape; white hamlets peer over granite cliffs at their reflection in tranquil seas. Everywhere, round or cubical lime-coated cottages, arches and terraces glisten in the sun. Cobbled alleys lead to upper levels gay with hanging gardens, sub-tropical shrubs and hedges of cactus. Huge windmills on windy points stretch out wide-sleeved arms; silver domes of Byzantine churches and their filigree towers can be seen for miles in the clear light.

To the south of the tideless Aegean, a group of about twenty-four islands is known as the Cyclades, from the Greek word *kyklos* (circle). The ancients believed that these islands lay in a rough circle around the holy island of Delos. Legendary birthplace of Apollo and his sister Artemis, Delos was the seat of one of Apollo's most famous temples. The tiny island—it is only a mile and a half long—was considered so holy that births and deaths were forbidden there. The nearby island of Rhenea was reserved for these natural events.

All the trade of the eastern Mediterranean world now flowed through the tiny harbor of Delos. This was a great period in the island's history. Elaborate houses, temples and places of assembly were built of marble, all along the waterfront. The tiny island is literally strewn with fallen columns, ruins of temples, theatres and imposing houses. The exteriors were plain, but the insides elaborately finished with stuccoed walls, mosaic floors, colonnaded courts, and large cisterns for rain water, since there was no water supply. Delos became also one of the big slave markets of Greco-Roman times. Eventually greed, racketeering and piracy brought excessive wealth and then destruction to the little island.

The 173-square-mile island of Naxos is the largest of the Cyclades, with numerous communities in the midst of lush verdure and vineyards. The most populous island is the 31-square-mile island of Skyros. Its capital, a glittering cubist town, spreads below a crumbling ancient acropolis, around the slopes of two conical hills. On one of these Rupert Brooke, the English poet, is buried. There are large flocks of goats on the island and a distinctive goat's-milk white cheese is produced here; also the delicious *loukoumia,* a Greek form of Turkish Delight. In 1922 an American orphanage was founded. Over seven thousand orphans have passed through this great institution. Both Naxos and Paros are familiar to every sculptor, for they are famous for their marble. The island of Melos, on the extreme southwest, is best known for the world-famous statue of Aphrodite, the Venus de Milo, which is now in the Louvre. Other famous sculptures were also unearthed here, including that of Poseidon in the Athens Museum, and the head of Asclepius in the British Museum. On Paros is the Byzantine Church of the Hundred Doors, said to have been founded by St. Helena, mother of Constantine. To the west of Paros, is tiny Antiparos, famous for its cave of stalactites.

The rallying point for Christian Greece—the modern Greek center of worship—is but a stone's throw from a classic shrine in the tiny island of Tenos, the Lourdes of the Mediterranean. At the extreme point of land guarding its main harbor, stands out the white Church of Evangelistria famous throughout the Orthodox world. It is built over a well, the spot where, in 1823, the miraculous ikon of the Virgin was found. Twice a year, on March 25th, the anniversary of the Greek Declaration of Independence, and August 15th, the Death of the Virgin, pilgrims from all over the Greek Orthodox world swarm to this church, to seek miraculous cures and pay homage to the ikon, supposedly painted by St. Luke himself.

One fascinating island is Santorini, a place of cliff dwellers. Its fame is mainly due to its spectacular volcanic structure and peculiar architecture. The cave houses are cut into chocolate brown lava cliffs, seared by many centuries of volcanic fires. Enormous cliffs rise from the little harbor of Skala to an elevation of about 800 feet. On the top is Thera, a sizable town, reached by a long zigzag climb up and around many hairpin turns. It is a dazzling town of flat-terraced, windowless houses, chapels, churches and windmills, hanging between blue sea and bluer sky.

Tenos, Skyros and Mykonos are the three most glittering gems of the Cycladic ring. These are islands of almost blinding whiteness. Though many of the buildings are actually of pastel colors, the intense sun and the lime mortar combined with the dry air, transform them into so many close-packed cubes of chalky whiteness. There are thousands of chapels and shrines; Mykonos alone has 350 chapels, chiefly erected by families or individuals in gratitude for some rescue at sea. On holidays, the air trembles to the sound of hundreds and hundreds of chapel bells.

Apart from the Cycladic group and the independent islands lying close to Asia Minor, there are two other principal groups, named from the way they are scattered like seeds. They are the Northern Sporades, and the Southern Sporades. Including big monster-like Eubœa, which is almost one with the mainland, the Northern Sporades form a broken bridge between Europe and Asia, leading to the entrance of the Dardanelles on the northeast. Clustered close to the southwest extremity of Asia Minor, the Southern Sporades include the Dodecanese, (twelve islands). Nearly all are rocky, and some, like Patmos, volcanic and treeless, for these barren ones have no springs or wells, and the people must depend on rock-hewn cisterns in which the winter rains are collected.

But Rhodes, the queen of the Dodecanese, whose soil according to Homer was watered by Zeus with rains of gold, has orchards, gardens, and pasture lands, balmy beaches and good-sized plains. Blood-red roses grow profusely everywhere; that's the reason it is called "the island of roses." Rhodian ships visited ports in Egypt and on the shores of the Black Sea, interchanging commodities of all parts of the ancient world, and returning loaded with goods and wealth. Rhodes undertook to police the seas and destroy piracy, and succeeded. Then was drawn up the famous Rhodian Sea Laws, a maritime code widely accepted by all seafaring peoples.

Rhodes became so powerful that it alone resisted all attacks of invaders. In 309 B.C., Demetrios, son of the King of Syria, who had besieged the city for a year and a half, was forced to retire; and in gratitude to the gods, the islanders erected the famous Colossos of

Rhodes. It was an enormous bronze statue of Apollo, one of the Seven Wonders of the ancient world. Ships passed in and out the harbor between the legs of the sun god. It was 105 feet tall, and was made by Chares of Lindos. In the year 224 B.C., along with the rest of the city it was destroyed by a violent earthquake, and was never again re-erected, by order of the oracle of Apollo at Delphi.

In 157 A.D., another earthquake reduced what was left of the once famous city into a pile of rubble. For hundreds of years it remained a poor and forgotten place but, lying on the path of Mediterranean trade routes, the island slowly regained some prosperity, and in 1097 we find Rhodian ships carrying supplies to the first Army of the Crusaders. Richard Cœur de Lion, in 1191, stayed in Rhodes with his English fleet, and Philip of France followed this example on his return trip from the Holy Land. On the 15th of August, 1309, after a three years' siege, the city of Rhodes was surrendered to the Knights of St. John, also known as the Knights Hospitalers. They turned the city into one of the strongest fortresses in the whole Levant. All about this beautiful island of roses, to this day, marble columns, Gothic houses, ruins of mighty fortresses, reminders of classical and Greco-Roman civilizations, exist side by side with 19th-century villas and modern houses.

The shore lines of the Aegean islands are scalloped with tiny inlets and bays. The ports are the center of each island's civic activity and economic life. The easterly Etesian winds circle the southern islands, making easy a round-trip journey by boat. The water never rises beyond its allotted domain; boats can enter or leave the harbors at any hour. If high waves sometimes occur, they are even, rhythmic and widely spaced rollers. The coastline is generally abrupt, clearly chiseled in granite cliffs.

When cruising caiques and boats with pilgrims or tourists arrive, there is great excitement at the port. Boatmen in tiny painted feluccas race to the ship's ladder to bring the passengers ashore. Boys and girls sell postcards, fruit and flowers. Native articles, expertly woven belts, bright rugs or colorful textiles of native wool, are put out on display.

Moored to the mole are strange craft of many sizes and colors. Fishermen's nets hang on walls and railings to dry in the sun. On this corner you see sponge-fishing boats, just in from a six months' trip to the Barbary Coast, laden with bright sea harvest. On another corner large power boats load a cargo of lemons or fruits in season. Nearby, from tiny skiffs, bronzed men and boys dive to search the bottom for rare-colored shells or for hiding octopus, a choice delicacy of the islanders. In the middle of the bay are moored the great-bellied, three- or four-masted caiques with countless ropes and yards, built to carry heavy loads to distant ports. These are beautiful, dignified ships, and can be seen from great distance coming into port with all sails set and swelling in the breeze. There are crescent-shaped, two-masted boats called *trehanteria* or racers, built to carry lighter loads faster to the mainland, and back. These are elegant, swift boats, whose hulls are gaily striped and whose prows are decorated with mythical monsters or mermaids.

The smell of oil and fish comes from a little canning factory nearby, while from another direction the smell of hot paint and tar from the shipyard. There is always the smell of drying herring and fish, paint and tar, and the smell of anchovies. But the aromatic smell of native wines is the strongest. Row upon row, wooden barrels line the walls of each little tavern, where seamen and sailors drink and sing, and often quarrel. And one always sees a surprising number of peaceful islanders simply sitting at windows and balconies, watching the changing shadows on the far-off mountains, or the changing colors of sky and sea.

Tens of thousands of Greece's people earn their living from the sea. All along this region of silver shores a floating and ever-sailing population is doing business. Greece has a flourishing merchant marine— seventh in the world before World War II. Greek ships ply mainly between foreign ports, as Greece's own foreign commerce is quite limited. Some of the most prosperous Greeks are the shipowners, their ships sailing under nearly every flag and often not visiting Greece at all.

Besides net fishing done along the coast, a good deal of offshore fishing is likewise carried on for weeks or even months at a time by open-sea boats employing mainly the *zoka*—four strong hooks fixed together and baited with a whole fish or octopus. No great bluefins, giant tunas or ponderous salmon are caught here. The fish of the Greek seas are small. Sturgeon do come to the Hellespont from the Black Sea during the spawning season, but virtually all the fishing industries of Greece deal with canning, salting, drying of mackerel and sardines caught in nets. There are of course quantities of olive oil, and the salt works produce more salt than can be used. It is always a surprising fact to strangers that Greece, with seas all round, must import cod and herring, chiefly from the United States. Moreover, Greece imports local fish from the Mediterranean countries, too! Why? Because, as with the land, the sea has been overharvested. Abuse of marine life in Aegean waters had in time the same results as neglect of the land: meager, decreasing yields. But now thanks to UNRA, to Marshall Plan assistance and technical advice, Greek fishermen have more than doubled the fifty-million-pound annual pre-war catches. ECA funds have been provided for fisheries surveys, for the stocking of lakes and lagoons, and transplanting into Greek waters and seas new types of fish from America.

An important occupation of the islanders is sponge fishing. The clear waters furnish the finest silky sponge specimens in the world. But again, centuries of harvesting have exhausted the once rich beds. So, farther and farther from home grounds the sponge divers spread, searching for new fertile grounds. Today their activities extend as far as Egypt, Crete, Tunisia and Tripolitana.

Greece herself has been the center of a major sponge industry through many centuries. Still today, come Epiphany Day (January 6th), when the waters are blessed by the priest, and a supply of water is drawn and stored for the whole year to be used in lustrations, purifications and baptisms, the quaint sponge fishing boats are blessed too, and husky sun-bronzed Dodecanesians, whose remote ancestors fought in the Trojan war, set sail for North African sponge grounds.

On the western coast of Greece, the Ionian Islands have long been called the "Isles of Enchantment." They look like illustrations for a fairy tale:—ethereal lights, silver-blue shadows, rocks rising out of a sea of luminous blue, the valleys aglow with roses, oleander and orange blossoms. Fruits and flowers abound in utmost profusion.

As a resort the richly wooded island of Corcyra (Corfu), the northernmost, situated close to the coast of Epirus, is the finest, attracting tourists and visitors the year round. It is easily accessible from continental Europe. The small plains and valleys are well cultivated and the hillslopes covered with olive, fig and cypress trees. Many olive trees are immense in size and centuries old. Poppies grow everywhere in Greece, but those of these islands are vividly painted in streaks of all colors! Magnolias, palms, bananas, eucalyptus and papyrus flourish in sheltered places.

The largest island in this group is Cephalonia, which probably owes its name to the mountains which rise abruptly from the sea, the highest peak being over five thousand feet. Argostoli, the main town, with a fine port, is the center of considerable trade in currants, main crop of these islands, oil and wines.

There is one other island—by far the largest in the Greek Archipelago. That is Crete, the southernmost point of Europe. Because it was the cradle of Greek civilization, it is there that our story of Greece must begin.

Chapter Three

PEOPLE OF THE LAND

As a UNIFIED government, Greece is a new nation, but its people are old—so old that in country districts they seem to harmonize and be one with the landscape. They are not very numerous. They never were. In their long and turbulent history, they were never more than eighteen million. They are only eight million now, and more than half of them—68 percent—are workers of the soil and the sea. The land has been ploughed and changed by many centuries of people who have lived and struggled to wrest subsistence from it. And the sea has been searched and sailed for whatever it could give, and the two hold the dead of many generations and are one again.

In the life of the Greek people, customs and tradition handed down through many centuries still are the basis of everyday life. From north to south, from east to west there is the same culture, language and religion. In everything the ancient is the background for the modern. The thought, the *ethos* of these people has been in good part shaped by the eroded, deforested hills, the crumbling masonry of old villages, the white temples in the sun.

How can a country so small have survived so many generations of invasion and occupation, and have retained its racial character, national identity, language and religion? The story of Greek civilization is a very long one, longer than that of any other people in Europe. It is really the story of one people preserving certain standards of behavior and aspiration through many political changes. This appears strange, at first, seeing how tiny the country is, few regions being more than five hundred miles apart. And stranger, when we know that the soil is the poorest in Europe. "Greece and poverty are twins," is a popular saying. Her per capita income amounts to less than one-tenth that of America. Why is that? Because of wars, for one reason. Greece is situated right in the path of the migratory impulses of many peoples and through many centuries was despoiled by invaders. But Greece is poor mostly because of lack of natural resources, water power, and extensive arable terrain.

But let us remember that this poor land is rugged with hills and almost everywhere close to the sea. Farmer, shepherd and seaman sometimes change occupation over night. Two-thirds of the people can see blue water from their windows. No country, in proportion to its size, has a longer naturally broken up coastline than Greece.

These characteristics of the landscape are favorable to the development of a strong and active race. Secluded mountain valleys and plains have fostered a spirit of individualism, independence and self-reliance. Navigation and all that relates to it: shipbuilding, commerce, fishing and emigration, is the traditional chief livelihood of the people. Limited areas of productive land, and lack of food and natural resources forced the Greek people to move outward. All over the Mediterranean world and the lands beyond they migrated, established trading posts and cities. Even to this day the people are scattered and many colonies are to be found beyond the borders of their native land. Rare are the families that haven't one or more members away from home most of the time. A dominant thought of many a Greek boy is where can he go to better his lot and that of his family.

Even though generally subtropical, the climate varies perceptibly from region to region. In the South, where the drought-resisting olive and vine grow, it is typically Mediterranean. In the North, where oak, chestnut and walnut thrive side by side with fruit trees, it is temperate, with extremes of cold in winter and heat in summer. A third type, the alpine, prevails in the higher plateaus among the mountains of both south and north. Here are forests and summer pastures.

This variety of climate over a small area results in a rather astonishing variety of crops. In the southwest and the Ionian Islands, the warmth favors the growth of near-tropical vegetation. Small banana and grapefruit trees grow side by side with the big citrus, lemon and almond. There are quince trees and currant vines. While snow glistens on the peaks of Mount Hymettus, below it on the plains of Attica oranges ripen. A most characteristic feature of the landscape is the profusion of wildflowers blooming in winter around the Acropolis. The almond tree is the first to burgeon early in the spring, and in many places in the very heart of winter. Farther south, Mount Taygetus may be snow-clad in late May or June, while on the plains of Messenia and Sparta, not far away, the dates ripen, and in Naxos the lemons and limes.

The towns are more numerous in the south, along the seaboard and the marginal strip between hills and sea. They are well chosen sites, opening into the world's maritime routes. Former culture, trade and traffic heads are now administrative and agricultural centers. As their names indicate, they are ancient towns. They appeared and disappeared many times; new structures rising on the remains of older ones again and again. Archæologists are uncovering layers of civilization here, one on top of another.

The peasant population is the backbone of Greece, and the country-side is dotted with picturesque villages and hamlets where these people live. They are located usually on a sunny slope or hillside, often on steep cliffs, so as to leave every possible acre of flat soil available for cultivation. They usually overlook a valley, vineyards and a river winding to the sea. A silver-domed and red-roofed Byzantine church on the height dominates the whole area. When the churchbell rings, its echo can be heard all round the countryside where people toil. The church is the soul and center of the village. The church and the school are closely related. The priest and the teacher are the most important persons in the village. The *kafenio*—coffee house—is the men's club, where one buys tobacco, drinks thick black coffee in demi-tasse, or smokes an *argile* (hubble-bubble water pipe) and talks politics. Womenfolk have their club at the village fountain, where gossip and laughter begin. Another familiar spot is the big communal oven built of bricks and stones, where housewives of the whole neighborhood bake bread, cakes and pastries. Holiday gatherings take place on the open-to-the-sky threshing floors where the stamping of grain is done. Here, on clear, warm holidays, celebrations and dances take place, with wine and music, and perhaps an open-air play.

Entire villages are built in a functional style of architecture, consisting of a cluster of stone houses, some topped by clay tile roofs. Nothing is big, imposing or complicated here. No congested areas, no "marginal black spots," no courts, no police, and no traffic problems. Each village is a "country" in itself, with its distinct kind of social life. A great many of these villages are composed of a number of families of the same surname. Blood ties bind the people; they are sacred. So people know each other; have known and are related to one another and are as one clan. Everybody feels entitled to know the business of the other; to share the joy or sorrow of everyone else in the village. Many transactions are carried on solely through a man's word of honor. It is far more binding than a written contract. A man's word is the man himself, his people, generations of people. This is peculiarly Greek.

Year in and year out, peasant life goes on as of old. Members of the same clan come and go, in the same village and the same house, much as the seasons come and go. Life is real and rolls naturally, leisurely in dawns and sunsets. Harvesting is followed by the vintage and the olive-picking seasons. Baptismal and marriage rejoicings are followed with burial rites and mournings. War clouds gather, time for tears; sunlight of peace dawns, time for laughter and dance. The plain homespun cotton or woolen everyday working dress is replaced by the silk-striped skirt and gold-embroidered jacket. Sequin necklaces and coin bracelets glisten and tinkle as the maidens join hands in a circle, and the white pleated *fustanella* whirls as men twirl and swing round and round dancing the ancient *syrtos*, "the eternal circle," the sacred Dithyramb, on the communal dancing floors.

No absentee landholders and no semi-feudal estates exist in Greece. The land belongs to all the people. Each family, no matter how poor, owns enough to live on—a vineyard, a garden, a corn patch, fruit and olive trees, a mule or a donkey, and goats or sheep. And each family owns its house. It passes from father to son. But good productive soil is scarce, and farm patches are small: three, five, ten acres at most. And even though Greece is predominantly agricultural, farming methods are as ancient as the land itself. In the plains where the flat land makes more extensive cultivation possible, American tractors, threshing, binding and other kinds of power-operated machinery do much of the backbreaking work. But in the steep mountainous areas and remote country where land is rocky and uneven, the ancient Homeric plow is still in use, drawn by ox or mule, terracing the small patch, season in and season out. Seeding is still done mostly by hand; cultivating by hoe; harvesting with the hand sickle. The soil is husbanded with great care. Yields are scanty.

The lack of fuel for fire, or of flour for bread is every peasant's constant spectre. Anything which will burn and is not needed for more important purposes is gathered and brought home. An everyday scene, anywhere in the countryside, is a line of donkeys or ponies laden with wood for hearth and stove. During the Nazi occupation a large number of these beasts of burden were taken from the people or killed, so now the burden of carrying home loads of faggots or drywood often is borne by women and children, who carry it on their backs.

In antiquity, Greece was better forested, and the soil more productive. But as the population increased, the people were forced to clear the land, to grow grain. They also depended on the forests for fuel and wood, because of lack of good coal and water power. So, big protective trees were cut, one after another. Centuries of deforestation, coupled with constant flock grazing on the tender sprouting shoots of young growing trees and forage plants, left the land barren and the soil exposed to driving winter rains. The springs dried up; the soil deprived of its natural protection and moisture lost its productivity, and much of it washed away. By the sixth century A.D., Greece was forced to import lumber for construction besides grain for bread. Still today, much of it is imported, since not even five percent of the country is forested.

Cover crop, the sowing of alfalfa, ryegrass or sweetclover, which not only would check erosion of hillsides, but would clothe the land with forage providing feed for the livestock, was not practised until recently. Nearly a fourth of Greece is now abandoned as unproductive. So heavy work is required to make the soil produce. The people have to work hard. They dig drains to combat erosion. Where the hills are lean and wan, the people build pockets of soil, clothe it, protect it with great care to make it bloom and yield. The peasants have at last learned to work with nature rather than try to outwit her.

There is no very clear-cut Greek type; the most striking feature of the face is an excessive breadth at the angles emphasizing the squareness of the jowl. The average Greek is of medium height, or—judged by American standards—short in stature. Although there are many fair Greeks, the majority are olive-skinned, dark-eyed. The women usually are raven-haired, almond-eyed, not unlike certain types found in classic statues. And they are as industrious as the men. They are always busy at the kitchen garden, or with distaff and spindle, embroidery or knitting. Through long winter nights they produce homespun, richly embroidered gowns, woollen costumes and house blankets which last a lifetime. The entire peasant family's clothing, from the hand-worked leggings worn in the highlands in winter, to sturdy gowns and head scarfs woven on the house loom, are designed and finished by the female members of the household. Women's styles have outlived many conquerors.

The Greek sense of family and filial devotion is strong. That family sense is perhaps the greatest stabilizer in the Greek social fabric. The Greeks also, as heirs to a vast cultural and spiritual tradition, are passionately proud of this heritage, and intensely aware of themselves as a particular people and a nation. Perhaps, because of this, they do not generally lend themselves to large collective enterprises; they are more successful and happier in personal ventures. Greeks, commercially gifted, are good traders and adventurers. They are fond of learning; education has always taken a prominent place in their lives. No titled nobility, no class distinction and no social aristocracy divide the people into castes or classes. Greeks are enthusiastic people in all things—but particularly as regards politics. They are seriously concerned with government, and the way it works. Two Greeks, they say of themselves, constitute a political argument; three Greeks, a political party. They are a peace-loving people, but their history reveals that they will fight to death over even comparatively minor issues.

One of Greece's principal exports is tobacco. More than 60,000 tons is produced yearly. The economy of modern Greece is dependent largely on trade with the outside world; and in the last quarter century, tobacco has become the most important export. In many areas of the country, tobacco has taken the place of olives and grapes. The finest quality is grown in the northern provinces of Macedonia and Thrace. Before World War II, tobacco was grown on a total area of about 233,000 acres, about four percent of the cultivated acreage of the country. Now tobacco production is fourth in importance, after cereals, olives and wines, and accounts for over thirteen percent of the total production. A familiar late-summer sight is a peasant cottage in the tobacco-growing areas of the sunny foothills, the eaves and rafters and all edges of the roof hung with long bunches of the drying leaves. In late fall the crop is carried in bullock carts to the warehouses to be re-sorted, graded, fermented and baled for shipment. In Greece there are many modern cigarette factories, with every provision for the health and comfort of the workers—most of whom are women.

The cities and villages of Greece have the look of antiquity upon them. Through the centuries the basic design of the Greek house has changed very little, except for the removal of the *hestia* or hearth from the center of the room to one side against the wall, and the addition of the chimney instead of the elliptical opening in the ceiling. The central feature of a Greek house still is the courtyard, open to the sky, usually paved with cobblestones. It is much used by the family and the domestic animals, especially in summertime. Whether it is the single-room peasant house or the multi-storied, castle-like house of the well-to-do, there is always one big room with a fireplace, which is the center of domestic life and which frequently combines the functions of dining-room, living-room and bedroom.

The goat is the national animal of Greece, but the most cherished is the cow, which is somewhat similar in type to the Jersey, only sturdier. It is cherished not primarily for the milk or the meat it gives, but for its strength and power in pulling the plough on these rocky farms. Domestic cattle are used also for stamping the grain. The donkey is another much used animal. There are practically no large herds of cattle in Greece, because of the scarcity of water and good pasture. But the goat is ever-present and everywhere. Before the Axis occupation of Greece in the last war, there were over five million goats.

The first note of the cuckoo and the answer of the nightingale is the call to harvest for all country people. The harvest season, mid-May to mid-July is a long outdoor festival of work, song, dazzling sunshine, golden sheaves and golden dust. Only the housewife stays home to bake the bread and the spinach-rice pie, to boil the freshly cut garden greens, and to make the garlic sauce for the baked codfish. Even those too old to walk are carried to the fields, placed near the harvesters in the shade of olive or pine trees, an earthen pitcher of water and a brightly decorated homespun blanket by their side to lie and watch the busy clansmen.

Men in working clothes of homespun linen, rawhide sandals held by thongs wound about their legs, black kerchiefs flat around their heads, and women in plain dress, wearing red or gray kerchiefs in the shape of helmets, are busy from sunrise to sunset. Row upon row the golden sheaves and the polished scythes gleam in the intense sunlight. Dark dots, swallows circle the azure sky. The voice of the cicada sounds continuously, monotonous and metallic.

Harvest processions are seen everywhere: bright blankets on pack saddles, white-kilted men astride mules, and women, perhaps with children cradled in their arms, on donkeys. The elderly women ride bridleless donkeys and sit busily knitting, never dropping a stitch. Barefoot boys run along the rocky track, followed by barking dogs; close behind are the goatherds and goats with tinkling bells, and then the cows and oxen. All follow the zigzagging ancient trails.

A familiar sight is the mid-summer drying of the small, black seed-less currant grapes, grown on the sunny foothills all around the coastal belt of the Peloponnesus and the Ionian Isles. About 170,000 acres are devoted to their cultivation. When ripe, the raisins are cut from the small shrublike vines, and are spread out on canvas sheets to dry in the sun. They remain on the canvas from a week to ten days, and are then carefully packed for export. Currants, so-called from Corinth, one of the principal currant-vine districts, have been exported to England to be put into English plum puddings, cakes and buns, ever since Queen Elizabeth's time.

Another very characteristic feature of the landscape is the mauve and silver-gray olive groves. Some of these trees are a thousand years old. One of the major industries of ancient Greece was the picking and pressing of olives and the marketing of olive oil. To the ancients, olive oil was indispensable. All athletes massaged their bodies with it before entering the contests of the gymnasiums. Attica was especially re-nowned for its olives. Hymettus honey and Athenian oil in graceful clay jars were sent all over the Mediterranean.

Olives are quite as valuable to Greece today. The ripe fruits gath-ered in late autumn are crushed in special presses and the oil extracted and refined. The best quality comes from the islands of Crete, Corfu and Mytilene. Much of it is exported. But great quantities are con-sumed at home. Nearly all Greek food is cooked in oil, for butter and other cooking fats are scarce. The finest eating olives come from Kalamata, and Amphissa near Delphi. The Sacred War between Philip of Macedon and the Phocians (338 B.C.) was brought about by the Phocians having used the sacred olive groves (belonging to the Delphic Oracle) for secular purposes, thereby rousing the anger of other states in the Delphian League, who called upon Philip to punish Phocis.

Country people live without sanitation, heat or running water. Rural areas are retarded, for the people are generally poor. Greece lacks good coal and coal oil. Although great quantities of lignite exist in several areas, there has been little planned utilization of it. One-fifth of the whole population has electricity, the lowest per capita consumption of electric power in Europe. Greece depends wholly for fuel and power upon imports of petroleum and coal. But as industry expands there will be much greater need for power, and electricity will be brought to more outlying communities.

A joint Greek-American program now calls for electrification and other projects designed to provide the people with heat, water, light and roads and the tourist with greater comfort. The development of water power will cut down the importation of fuel and will aid agricultural areas by flood control. Drought threat to the valleys and plains will be overcome by irrigation.

Today the cities and larger towns of Greece are overcrowded. People have been flocking in from rural areas by tens of thousands, mainly from the northern regions, refugees from World War II and from the Civil Conflict just ended. Victims of the war between the National Army and the Communist-led guerrillas, a tenth of the total population, had been forced to leave their country homes and to seek security and protection in the towns. They threw up temporary communities on the outskirts of towns, living in tents or crude shacks, trying to keep their families together and existing on meager amounts of food and clothing provided by the government and their American friends acting through various relief agencies. Greece has always had some of her people return as refugees from neighboring regions, where they may have lived for centuries. Wars and the rise of nationalism forced many of them to return to the mainland poverty-stricken, clutching their few possessions in their hands. But the victims of the Nazis and the Civil conflict which followed were the most pitiful. Many, still, with their draft animals killed, their working tools stolen, and their villages in ruins, are hopefully waiting to return to their former homes. The result has been an acute congestion in cities, causing poverty, overcrowding and malnutrition.

Hammering and builders' voices are heard everywhere in Greece today, and particularly in the cities. Urban life is cluttered and chaotic, as there is so much change. In the streets are people from all parts of the world: American visitors and business men wearing shoes manufactured in New England walk alongside simply attired natives, or shepherds dressed in pleated woollen kilts, skullcaps and sandle-like shoes, called *pinges,* with huge white or red pompons.

The public markets are noisy and busy. Open-air stands spread for blocks and display anything from handmade pottery and baskets, to saints' ikons and turtledoves. Articles of food are spread among kitchenware and clothing. Most of the Greek merchants are also farmers. Greece is a land of individual industries. A market is a labyrinth of tiny shops and stands where each merchant makes what he sells. Peasant women in brightly embroidered jackets and billowing petticoats trade with fashionable women. Barefoot boys dart about, in ragged but colorful clothes. Vendors shout their wares. The air reeks with herbs, leather, garlic and fruit. And the sound of bargaining voices is almost deafening. The Greek people delight in haggling over a bargain, as they do over an idea.

The houses of the North are tall, strong and remarkably well built, for the winters are long, cold and damp. These houses are planned to give the occupants maximum comfort in winter and maximum sun and air in the summer. A house of people of means is usually three-storied, two stories of stone surmounted by a third of lime-coated wood. The lower stories are solid stone, often constructed with the purpose of withstanding attack, which gives the general appearance of a castle. With many rows of windows covered with strong wooden shutters and big balconies which take the place of sun decks in the summer, these houses have a unique and picturesque style.

Winter living quarters are in the middle story. A wooden balcony, two to four feet in height runs along the entire length of the main room, and serves as sleeping quarters when carpets and mattresses or homespun blankets are spread by the housewife. The ground floor is cellar and storeroom, with rows of wooden wine barrels along the wall, and boxes and jars for storing provisions. A primitive underground cooler preserves meat and other perishable food. If there are no outside stables, part of this ground floor houses the livestock during cold winter days.

Summer quarters are on the top floor. A closed balcony, used as guest room, is usually adjoined by several smaller rooms. On this floor is the dining-room with couches on its raised border on which visitors and guests recline while dining, drinking or talking. Often it is quite luxuriously furnished and beautifully decorated. It is spacious, with innumerable earthenware jugs and plates or engraved copper utensils. The handmade pottery still preserves many of the traditional shapes and patterns which have been handed down from ancient times. Wooden walls and ceilings are sometimes adorned with rich carvings.

There is a variety of exterior forms of architecture: overlapping roofs, terraces and closed balconies, with small fruit trees, kitchen-garden plants, jars spilling over with vines relieving the patterns of masonry.

The house of a poor villager is usually just one big room with a fire-place at one side and a wooden partition made of deep drawers. One half of the room shelters the animals. In the drawers grain and other crops are stored. The front yard is the summer living quarters shaded with vines and fruit trees. Small garden plots, piles of logs and faggots are all around. Here on mellow summer and autumn nights neighbors gather and children sit under the stars listening to *yaya* (grandmother) or the village storyteller retell old folk stories or invent new ones.

In the country and in small towns there are always many small gardens, for markets are found only in cities; each country family grows its own fruit and vegetables. There is no uniformity about them. They pop up anywhere and are not fenced. The vegetable gardens belong to the women. The orchards belong to the men. The tidy orchards and gardens near the river are carefully planted, the fruit trees pruned and sprayed.

The people of Greece are simple in their needs, thrifty and self-reliant. They live on a very plain diet. Homebaked wholewheat or corn bread is eaten three times a day, with each meal. Bread, wine and olives, hard white goat cheese, vegetables and fruit, make a meal for the average family. Fruit is abundant and wild succory, dandelion, rocket and other greens which we seldom use or regard only as weeds, are esteemed as ingredients in salads, both raw and cooked. Meat was always scarce in Greece. Centuries of meat scarcity has made the people near-vegetarian; and what meat they do have, apart from dried fish, is almost exclusively lamb or kid.

From one end of Greece to the other there is no very great difference in the way people live, work and play. Even in the cities, one is aware of the typical agrarian pattern of life just outside the town. Farmers frequently come into town, rub shoulders with fishermen, sailors, travelers. This, and the smallness of Greece, has given to its people something of a cosmopolitan viewpoint and kept even the poor shepherds and farmers from being ingrown and petty in thought. Greece is still a crossroads and a meeting place. The influx of nearly a million and a half Greek refugees from Anatolia in 1922, and the continuous trickle of returning Greek-Americans in the last half century, has far surpassed in numbers all the migrations of the past.

Chapter Four

THE LEGACY OF OLYMPUS

A SINGLE curious fact makes the story of Greece different from that of any other nation. All countries have their periods of great development and progress, as had Greece; and all countries, at one time or another, have produced great poets, philosophers, scientists, artists. But from no other land has there come such a stream of legend embodying the truths of man's existence and struggle and aspiration. Going back into the days before recorded history, these legends took on so many aspects of wisdom and poetry that they have kept alive, down through the ages and for all of the Western world, an awareness of moral and æsthetic values that has helped man immeasurably. One might say that the Greeks were the first to create and believe in "ideals." Moreover, they expressed these ideals in such powerful images and unforgettable stories as to fashion a legacy which has enriched and ennobled all peoples. You can scarcely think of Greece without remembering Zeus, the supreme god and final authority, or Heracles, type of masculine prowess and courage, or Aphrodite, the personification of pure beauty, or perhaps most wonderful of all— Athena, who stands for serene intellectual truth, unswayed by any personal passion, grief or desire.

To understand Greece, we must know not only how the Greek people live, and their history, but what is their outlook upon life, their temperament and spirit. The legends, like the famous plays of Aeschylus, Sophocles and Euripides, and the wonderful classic Greek statues, give us a very clear idea of how the Greeks saw themselves and the world around them. Many centuries have passed since the high period of ancient Athens, and, by admixture of many other invading peoples since then, the Greek racial type has certainly changed—but the ideals have not greatly changed, nor the pattern of social life and activity which brought about those ideals.

The early Greek people were "humanists"; that is, they put the concerns of human beings and the study of human nature first. Their gods were made in human shape—only more powerful and more beautiful. Their landscape of bright skies and blue sea, of green hills and valleys, was peopled with godlike beings. Each kind of country—mountains, plains, rivers, woods, had its special kind of presiding gods or half-gods—nymphs, fauns, bacchantes, nereids. The winds, the storms, the influences of day and of night were all personified and held in reverence. The waters of the Mediterranean sheltered the crystal palaces of Poseidon; Mt. Helicon became the abode of the Muses; Mt. Parnassus was sacred to Phœbus Apollo, the glorious sun god; and Olympus, the highest mountain by far, was the home of the supreme deities.

This was all a poetic and outward-looking concept of life. It was a worship of nature and man's part in nature. Hence, even though the gods were personifications of natural phenomena, they were like human beings in bodily form and in their needs and desires. They rejoiced and suffered, like man. They had problems to solve, tasks to fulfill. They were born, and married—but death never came to them. They were loftier beings, superior in power, beauty and skill. And they represented the ideal perfection of spirit and body to be sought by all people.

The great number of gods was the result of an attempt to create order out of a seemingly chaotic nature, to make a complete and understandable system of the relation of one natural force to another and of their significance to man.

People looked up to the mysterious cloud-capped summits of Mt. Olympus, and imagined seeing there, under the arch of heaven, the gleaming city of their gods. It was made the central point of the earth's surface. The cloud-gate of the celestial city was guarded by the Hours or Seasons. They opened it or closed it, to permit the passage of the gods in their frequent visits to earth, and to receive them on their return. On the topmost peak stood the Acropolis-like great hall, where the Olympic Council met when summoned by Zeus. Here the gods feasted or discussed the affairs of heaven and earth, while the Muses sang to the accompaniment of Apollo's lyre, and Hebe, the goddess of youth, poured nectar, nourishing the divine ichor flowing in the gods' veins. Ambrosia was served at the banquets, and the nostrils of the gods were filled with the rich odor of sacrifices offered by pious people on Earth.

On a golden throne sat Zeus and Hera, his wife. About them assembled the other ten gods: Poseidon, ruler of the seas; Phœbus, the sun god, patron of music, poetry and eloquence; Ares, god of war; Hephæstos, god of fire and artistry; Hermes, the herald, the messenger and patron of trade; Athena, goddess of civilization, learning and art; Artemis, the moon goddess, twin sister of Phœbus Apollo; Aphrodite, goddess of beauty and love; Hestia, goddess of domestic life; and Demeter, goddess of the harvest. Besides the twelve greater gods, there were many lesser divinities of heaven, earth, sea and the underworld: Eros, son of Aphrodite, small but mighty god of love with bow and arrow; the Muses, Graces and Furies; Pan, son of Hermes and a dryad, god of the wood, of flocks and shepherds; the Satyrs, the Sirens, and many nature spirits: Nereids, Nymphs and Oreads.

The busiest of the gods was Hephæstos, the blacksmith. Though slow and lame, he worked with great energy. He built the palaces of the gods and fashioned their shields and spears, the sceptre and the thunder-bolts of Zeus; the arrows of Apollo and Artemis; the breastplate of Heracles, the arrows of Eros. He helped at Athena's birth by cleaving Zeus' head with an axe, out of which Athena sprang agleam with panoply of war, and brandishing her spear.

One of the major earthgods was Dionysos, god of the vine, the drama, animal life and vegetation, promoter of civilization and wise lawgiver. Dionysos was crowned with vine-leaves and rode a panther, and his attendants were male field and woodland deities.

The three just and wise judges of the lower world of Hades were sons of Zeus: King Minos of Crete, his brother Rhadamanthus, and Aiakos, the righteous king of the island of Aegina.

There were three generations of gods. The first was that of Uranos (Heaven) and Gæa (the Cosmos), when the solar system was created; the second, that of Chronos (Time) and Rhea (Mother Earth), when the generation of the gods of Olympus was created; and the third that of Zeus and Hera, who are the founders of Greek mythology. The third generation was headed by three god-brothers: Zeus, Poseidon and Hades. Hera, the female force in nature, as wife of Zeus, links the gods with mankind.

The early Greek people knew no hell, nor heaven; only this earth existed for them. Olympus was their heaven and the underearth darkness their hell. And the earth was one and flat and round; a disk whose central point was in their own country. Near and far were counted from Delphi. The earth was divided into two equal parts by the Sea, as the Mediterranean was known. Circling the earth flowed the stream of Ocean, a great, mysterious and shoreless river, which moved in a steady current and fed the Sea and the rivers. Beyond those lands to which Greek enterprise and colonization penetrated, lay lands inhabited by one-eyed giants and monsters, and a race of tiny strange Pygmies. They imagined that to the north lived a happy race of people called the Hyperboreans, enjoying everlasting bliss. To the south lived the "blameless Ethiopians," a happy people, loved by the gods who visited them and shared their banquets. To the west lay the Elysian Fields or Island of the Blest, where those who had led noble lives were admitted to live eternally in calm happiness.

Uranos ruled in constant fear of his own children, the one-eyed Cyclopes and the hundred-handed giants. When at last he drove them back into the earth, Gæa in her distress called upon the Titans for deliverance. Obedient to his mother's call, Chronos, the youngest, greatest and craftiest, attacked Uranos and, having maimed him with a sickle, seized his power. Chronos, with his sister-wife Rhea, ruled the world for incalculable ages; but since he had been told that a son would overthrow his rule, as he had overthrown that of his father, he swallowed his own children, destroying whatever he brought into existence. Time destroys all that it creates. Thus Demeter, Hestia, and Hera, Poseidon and Hades came to the light only to be devoured by their father Chronos. But when Zeus, the sixth child was born, instead of the child, Rhea gave Chronos a swaddled stone, which he swallowed. The infant Zeus was kept for safety in the Diktean cave in Crete, where he was nursed by the nymphs, Adrastea and Ida, and nourished on honey and milk of the goat Amalthea, while the Curetes— mountain spirits—drowned his cries by clashing spears on their shields.

Zeus, when grown, with the help of his grandmother Gæa, forced Chronos to disgorge the five children he had swallowed and the stone, which was placed in the oracle at Delphi. He then declared war upon him. The gods fortified themselves on Mt. Olympus and the Titans on Mt. Othrys opposite Mt. Olympus. Ten years the struggle lasted without ceasing. The rugged mountains of Thessaly and the jumbled rocks and cliffs still bear witness to the fury of that conflict. Victory wavered in the balance. Again, acting on his grandmother's advice, Zeus released from their prison under earth, the one-eyed Cyclopes, and the hundred-handed giants. Now, armed with the thunderbolts given him by the Cyclopes and aided by the giants, Zeus struck until he gained victory. Those Titans who had aided him with Chronos in the conflict were buried deep in Tartarus, as far below earth as earth is below heaven.

The three god-brothers now divided the world. Zeus was chosen supreme sky-god, ruler of earth and heaven. When Zeus nodded, all the Olympians trembled. Poseidon was lord over the waters, and Hades of the dominion of the dead. Atlas, son of the Titan Iapetos, who had sided with Chronos in the war with Zeus, was doomed eternally to hold the heavens on his shoulders. But to his brothers Prometheus and Epimetheus, who espoused the cause of the gods for law and order among gods and men, greater dignity and broader powers were delegated. To Prometheus (Forethought), gifted with prophetic wisdom, was given the power of creating man. Epimetheus (Afterthought) created all the animals and provided them with the necessary faculties for their protection and preservation. To some he gave the gift of courage, swiftness, strength, sagacity; to others, scales, wings, claws or a shelly covering.

Prometheus molded out of clay a nobler animal than these. He shaped Anthropos (man) in the image of the gods and gave him an upright stature, so that while the other animals turn their faces toward earth, man gazes on the stars. Then, when he had created man, Prometheus gave to him the greatest possible help, the precious gift of fire! He ascended to heaven, lighted his torch at the chariot of the sun, and brought down fire to man. With that, man was raised above all other animals and was enabled to forge tools and weapons, to win earth's secrets and treasures and to develop commerce, science and the arts. Fire was the means and symbol of civilization.

But Prometheus fell under the displeasure of Zeus when he stood forth the champion of man against the gods. It was at an age—the Silver Age—when, Hesiod tells us, the altars of the gods were neglected and the deities were denied their due. Zeus had grudged mortals the use of fire, and was in fact planning their destruction and the creation of a new race. Now gods and man were in dispute at Sicyon concerning the prerogatives of each. At this joint meeting it was to be determined what part of beasts offered in sacrifice was due to the gods and what to men. Prometheus, by an ingenious trick, attempted to settle the question in favor of man. He cut up an ox, dividing it in two portions. In one was the lean flesh surmounted with the entrails; and in the other the bones wrapped temptingly in fat. He then offered Zeus his choice. And though aware of the intended deceit, Zeus chose the bones and the fat, because he intended to punish Prometheus and his creation, man, and accordingly deprived man of fire.

Prometheus, desperate, regained fire for mankind by stealing it, in a tube, from the hearth of Zeus in heaven. For this defiance and for his unselfish devotion to mankind, Prometheus was chained by Zeus to a rock on Mt. Caucasus, where an eagle ever preyed upon his liver, yet succeeded not in consuming it, for it ever grew again. This torment could have been brought to an end at any time by telling Zeus a secret which Prometheus alone possessed, and which involved the stability of the god's throne. But the Titan bore his torture for uncounted ages. At last Prometheus was set free by Heracles, son of Zeus, who as part divine and part human, became the mediator between man's benefactor and the gods. Once again Prometheus was brought to Olympus and restored as prophet to the gods.

Because of the theft of fire, Zeus devised evil against man as well. This was done in the shape of a woman, fashioned in Heaven, with all the gods contributing something to her perfection. Though Prometheus had warned his brother Epimetheus never to accept anything from Zeus, Epimetheus foolishly accepted this woman, Pandora, "gift of the gods," brought to him by Hermes. Besides all other gifts, the gods gave Pandora a casket with the command on no account ever to open it. But curiosity was too strong. Pandora's mind was on the casket, until she at last raised the lid! The instant she did that out flew a multitude of winged little creatures and fluttered all about; pains, sins, diseases, plagues, envy, spite, jealousy and what not, scattering themselves far and wide, so that no one on earth could escape them. Before Pandora could replace the lid only Hope was left behind within the mouth of the casket, and never flew out.

The world now was peopled. The first age, the Age of Gold, begun in the reign of Chronos, was an age of innocence and happiness. Mortal men lived like gods, knowing neither pain nor toil. Though there was no authority to threaten, punish or enforce the law, truth and justice prevailed. There were no spears, swords or implements of war and only peace and goodness were in the hearts of men. The generous earth bore fruit of herself without ploughing or sowing. Perpetual spring reigned. The men of this age never grew old and feeble, and when death came to them, it was like peaceful, uneventful sleep, in which, unseen by mortal eyes, they still attended men as monitors and guardians. Next came the Silver Age, inferior to the first. Zeus shortened the spring, and divided the year into seasons. Crops would no longer grow without planting. This was a race of manly men, but insolent and impious. When they died, Zeus made them ghosts of the underworld, but withheld immortality from them. Next came the Bronze Age, when men insolently delighted in war and strife. Of bronze were their hearts, of bronze their weapons, of bronze were their homes, and the good deeds of this age were undone by the very inventions and creations of the people. Last of all was the Age of Iron, of which Hesiod says: "Mankind in the Iron Age will never cease by day or by night for weariness and woe, until the race ends." Family love was lost and friendship and the rights of hospitality forgotten. Honor and truth were replaced by fraud and violence; might was right. The gods one by one abandoned the earth and withdrew to Olympus, with Astræa, goddess of innocence and purity, following last.

When Zeus, then, saw how utterly wicked men had become, he resolved to destroy all the people of the earth and provide a new race, unlike the present, which should be worthier of life, and more reverent. To the council summoned in heaven, destruction by fire seemed too dangerous, lest a conflagration might overwhelm Olympus itself. So he proceeded to drown the world. He summoned the south wind which brings the rains, to open all the sluices of heaven. He called on Poseidon to let loose all the waters of the world. A tremendous downpour began. In the cataclysmic rush of waters Europe was separated from Asia.

The great flood spread over fields and hills, swept away whole cities, destroyed flocks, crops, temples, fortifications—every vestige of human life. Everywhere there was one boundless ocean now. The human race perished—all but Deukalion, son of Prometheus, and Pyrrha, daughter of Epimetheus. These two just and good persons, taught beforehand by Prometheus, the wise Titan, had fashioned a great chest, in which they took refuge, bringing with them all that was necessary for life.

In the limitless ocean Parnassus alone, of all the mountains, over-topped the water, and there, after floating nine days, did the chest touch ground. Zeus looked down from Olympus and saw that all the violent race of men had been swept off the face of the earth except for this pair of devout worshippers. He caused the sea to return to its

allotted shores, and the rivers to their channels. Then Deukalion and
Pyrrha stepped out of the chest and beheld a wasted and unpeopled
earth. Silence and loneliness brooded everywhere. Entering a temple,
defaced with slime, they approached the unkindled altar and fell pros-
trate, praying for guidance. The oracle made answer that they should
cast behind them the bones of their mother. They heard the words
with astonishment. Pyrrha first spoke: "We cannot obey; we dare not
profane the remains of our parents." But knowing that the god could
never command them to commit impiety by disturbing the tomb of
their mortal parent, Deukalion resolved the true meaning of the command. The earth is the great parent, the Mother of all, and her stones
are her bones. With heads bowed reverently and veiled faces, they
unbound their garments, and picking up stones, cast them behind them,
as they descended the mountain. Those thrown by Deukalion assumed
the forms of men, those that Pyrrha threw, the forms of women. And
the earth would be repeopled now.

Deukalion and Pyrrha became the parents of a new race, the race
to which we belong. Hellen was their son; and Hellen had three sons:
Ion, Aeolos and Dorus. This triad constitutes the three main ancestral
tribes of Greek people: Ionians, Aeolians and Dorians, bound by a
common nationality, language and religion, and common institutions,
oracles and athletic games. Is it at all surprising that even today the
Greek people with pride call their country Hellas, land of Hellen, and
themselves Hellenes?

Chapter Five

THE DAWN OF GREEK HISTORY
(3,500-1,000 *B.C.*)

IN THE LAST quarter of the 19th century, Dr. Heinrich Schliemann first undertook the excavation of Troy, on the Asia Minor coast, and Mycenæ on the mainland of Greece. He amazed the whole world with his discoveries. He recovered relics of the days of Homer, hitherto known only in literary descriptions and supposedly semi-mythical. Later Sir Arthur Evans of Oxford made even more astounding discoveries. On Crete he uncovered the palace and the city of Knossos (near modern Candia), bringing to light a still more ancient civilization.

The many tablets and clay labels found in the Cretan ruins point to long records or inventories kept by a strong centralized government. Bronze was the basic metal of this civilization, which emerged from more primitive stages and reached its height between 1,900 and 1,600 B.C.

Excavation continued in other parts of Crete, bringing to light smaller palaces and villas. It soon appeared that in Crete there had lived a rich seafaring people highly cultured, and with much artistic and architectural skill. Sir Arthur Evans gave this civilization the general name Minoan, after the legendary Cretan King Minos, and divided it into three periods: Early Minoan (3,000-2,200 B.C.); Middle Minoan (2,200-1,600 B.C.), and Late Minoan (1,600-1,100 B.C.).

The Greek people believed that there was a king called Minos, and some even claim there was a whole dynasty of kings bearing the name. We do not know yet, but we do know that four thousand years ago life in Crete was startlingly modern. Here was centered a mighty sea power with commercial contacts and trading posts on the mainland,

Troy on the Hellespont, Cyprus, Syria and Egypt, and settlements farther west in Italy, Africa and Spain. Its wares were to be seen all over the Mediterranean world. But what is more important is that the Minoans had developed a sufficiently high civilization to form a well-ordered state based on man-administered laws. Crete, at this earliest time, was so powerful that other cities from far and wide paid tribute to her kings. One of these cities was Athens, which sent every ninth year a tribute of seven youths and seven maidens, according to legend, to be sacrificed to the man-bull called Minotaur, kept in the Labyrinth of Knossos, King Minos' palace, built by the master Cretan craftsman named Dædalus.

This is the ancient story of King Minos, the Labyrinth and the man-bull, which came to us as a myth and was thought to be just a myth and nothing more, until archæologists digging into the soil of Crete did find this big palace whose ground-plan and imposing ruins and treasures indicate that it really was one of great wealth and splendor. Built on the slope of a hill, it covered six acres, and in some places was four or five stories high. It had spacious courts, pillared halls and luxurious fittings. An impressive staircase of five flights of broad easy steps led to upper floors. The whole is so big and complicated that it does give the impression of a labyrinth.

The palace walls were decorated with wonderful frescoes, which depict in charming fashion, vivid color and great skill, scenes from Cretan daily life. They are so fresh and so vivid that they give the impression of having been drawn recently!

The Cretan artists did their designing with a brush while the plaster on the wall was still wet. They painted in vivid colors for movement and action. They loved nature. Animals, rare fishes and birds, white lilies against red backgrounds, are the subjects of these frescoes, and more rarely, crowds of people. Men are generally painted red or dark, and women white, with very narrow waists for both. These art objects give us a good idea as to how the people looked, how they dressed and how they lived. Men had long black hair, classical features and high skulls, types that are still to be seen on the island today. Other frescoes depict scenes of griffin-drawn chariots; hounds attacking boars, charging bulls, circus, ball playing, boxing, wrestling and leaping. Others show blue monkeys peering through papyrus flowers, partridges and hoopoes, or monkeys gathering saffron in a meadow filled with crocuses. Perhaps the most beautiful is the stucco relief of a priest-king known as the Cup-bearer, found in the palace of Knossos. It shows a tall, dark-haired, handsome youth, with an engraved signet on his wrist, advancing slowly in a dignified posture, and carrying with both hands a long, pointed vessel of a shape often found in Crete.

The bull was sacred and occupied a place of honor in the life and customs of the ancient Cretans. Scenes on frescoes, carved gems and bronzes found there illustrate one of the favorite pastime sports of the Cretans—that of bull-grappling. They had other sports: bull-leaping, wrestling, boxing, ball games, dancing and various armed combats, but bull-grappling was the favorite.

We can imagine a day of sports in ancient Crete. The great flagged court of the palace of Knossos is crowded with five or six hundred spectators, standing around the wide flight of steps leading up to the palace balcony, where groups of elaborately coiffured ladies dressed in long flounced skirts, their hair in ringlets, watch the contests. In the royal box high above the court the king raises his hand and the games start. The preliminaries include a ball game, boxing, and a wrestling match. But the king loves to watch the bull-grappling contest, his son or even his daughter may be taking part in it, and it is a contest for the fearless and the brave. It is not a bullfight, where the object is the death of the animal. No! This is a sport in which a high degree of skill, acrobatic agility and daring is displayed. Now a youth seizes the bull by the horns and vaults, or turns a sort of handspring over its back, landing behind the bull as it passes, and if more brave, lies on it, back to back. Then, with a quick somersault lands clear behind the bull, while another youth catches him or leaps on the bull. But this is not a game for boys only, girls take part in this dangerous sport. Suddenly there is an accident, the youth misses his hold and is thrown on the ground or even on the bull's horns and is wounded. Blood drips as he falls, but another youth is ready to leap in and take his place.

The king had many other interests than sports and dances. One part of the palace consisted of magazines where immense jars stood filled with oil, wine and grain. Here also were the workshops, the arsenal, and the potters' studios, where the famous Cretan vases were made. The storerooms were full of jars, some so big that one could easily hide in one of them.

The Cretan people enjoyed town life. There were ninety prosperous cities. Knossos alone and the nearby port had a population of 100,000. But the bulk of the people lived in settlements, with houses of two and three stories built around a court. Aqueducts, an excellent drainage system, paved roads and bridges were part of the city plan. The life was simple, but gay and carefree. The men were simply dressed in loin-cloths. But the women wore elaborate and astonishingly modern fashions; both sexes used much jewelry. Children had their pull-carts and other toys. The people were busy in workshops and olive presses, at weaving and dyeing cloth, or fashioning gold ornaments and bronze-inlaid armor. Others manned the great fleets or hunted, and tilled the land.

Reading, writing and arithmetic were known to the Minoan people. They wrote on various durable objects, more frequently on seal-stones. Crete had cleared the seas of pirates and sent settlers to many parts of the Aegean. It was a state based on man-administered laws, probably the first ones. So sure were the rulers of their power and prestige that they did not even fortify their many cities and towns, for they trusted to the fear of their name, their great navy, and the surrounding sea to protect them.

But Crete did have an enemy, a bad one, who struck suddenly. Crete was subject to earthquakes then as she still is. Around 1,400 B.C. the island suffered a terrible catastrophe, so sudden and so complete, that it never again fully recovered. Just what it was is not known. People were cut off in the midst of their daily tasks; and religious ceremonies in progress left unfinished, the oil jars filled for this purpose left standing there. Fire broke out and became a conflagration in many places. What happened? Was it an earthquake or an invasion? We are not sure.

But though Crete was destroyed, its culture and influence were already stamped on the life of all the people of the Aegean world. Her gods were enthroned on Olympus.

With the decline of Crete, a new era began. People from Thessaly and Bœotia had colonized Chios and Lesbos and the adjoining mainland. This was called Aeolis. The Ionians (Athenians) from central Greece had colonized the Cyclades and a strip along the Asia Minor coast. This is called Ionia. It extended from Attica to Eubœa, across the islands to the central Asia Minor coast and bordered on the great kingdom of Lydia. The most famous city was Miletus, which soon became the center of trade and culture. Ionia was rich; its climate well adapted for trade. And it was in Ionia that two worlds and two ways of life, the east and the west, the Oriental and the Greek were molded into one.

The people of this period lived in walled hill-towns. On the top of the hill was a palace where the rulers lived. Many Greek cities and towns had a fortified hill, or *acropolis,* and these places came to be devoted to the gods and heroes of the state. Two of the earliest and best fortified towns were Mycenæ and Tiryns, in the Argive plain. Little Tiryns by the sea in northeast Peloponnesus was of great antiquity, its strong walls in places fifty-five feet thick, formed of huge blocks. These are the famous Cyclopean Walls, the oldest monuments in Greece.

Around 1,500 B.C., a powerful dynasty centered here. This was the Mycenæan or "Shaft-Grave-Dynasty," so named from the beehive tombs, cut vertically in the rock of the acropolis, where the kings are buried. The rulers of Mycenæ were of northern stock. They brought with them their own religion, a new and richer Greek speech and many of their own traditions, such as buildings with pitched roofs, instead of the traditional Mediterranean flat-terrace type. Judging from the gold burial masks found in the royal tombs, they were stern, bearded men of dignity and power. And the greatest wonders of their culture are the tombs, the Treasury of Atreus, and the fortress of the acropolis with its carved Lion Gate.

The greatness of Mycenæ was partly due to its ideal location. On a knob in the pass between two mountains, it dominated the Argive plain and commanded the trade-routes west to the Gulf of Corinth and south to Argos and Tiryns. Mycenæ, Tiryns, Cleonæ, Argos and other hill-towns combined in a mighty federation under the leadership of the Mycenæan kings.

To the northeast of the Aegean was another great and famous city called Troy, strongly walled and set on the Hellespont, where Europe and Asia meet. Troy, the northernmost Minoan outpost, was even better situated than Mycenæ, on the route of traffic crossing between Europe and Asia, and between the Aegean and the Black Seas. Both land and sea harvest could easily be had here. It was the toll taken from the long Mediterranean waterway sea traffic which made Troy the richest of all towns in the Aegean world. It was well walled and adorned with temples and towers gleaming in the sun, which gave it another name, Ilion, meaning city of the sun. Priam was Troy's king; Hector and Paris were his sons; brave and strong were the Trojans.

But the Mycenæans were bold adventurers by sea, constantly pressing for new trade outlets. Both cities were at the height of power and both were seeking to expand. And the two came to a clash. Under the leadership of Agamemnon of Mycenæ, and his brother Menelaus, King of Sparta, a hundred ships sailed across the Aegean from the little harbor of Aulis in Bœotia, and anchored before Troy in the summer of 1,194 B.C.

For ten long years the Achæan Greeks fought before the walls of Troy, and not until the tenth year were they able to enter the city, through the ruse of the wooden horse. Ilion was set on fire; the people were taken slaves and the city left in ruins. But Aeneas, chief of the Trojans, who escaped, in search of a new home, finally landed in Hesperia, now called Italy, where he founded a city near the coast, a few miles south of the Tiber. Vergil in his *Aeneid* tells the story of the Trojans and their wanderings in search for new homes. Homer tells the whole story of the Trojan war in the *Iliad*.

The Mycenæans were not left long in peace after the Trojan war. Now new invaders from the north, called Dorians (Spearbearers), came pouring down by land and sea, conquering and destroying as they came. They had no trouble conquering, because they came with superior weapons and implements made of iron. The Mycenæans used the softer metal, bronze. The Dorians were one of the Greek clans pushed down from farther north into central Greece in prehistoric times. Herodotus says the Dorians were Macedonians.

The Dorians did not come alone. Other northern clans joined them. They overran the tremendous fortifications of Mycenæ and Tiryns, and conquered Crete and Melos. They occupied Corinth and nearly all of the Peloponnesus. Argos was made a Dorian city, and Sparta became the capital of all their land.

The Dorian invasions caused a greater cycle of displacements; people were again in search of new homes. Many Mycenæans settled in nearby Attica, round Athens and the island of Eubœa. Others joined the Athenians in their eastward migration to Ionia, bringing with them their language, religion and traditions, and their stories of the Trojan war. Among them were bards and rhapsodists who, traveling from place to place at the feasts of the chieftains or the courts of the rulers, sang the brave deeds of heroes on both sides in the Trojan war. One of these bards was Homer, the greatest of all.

The Dorian invasions mark the great transitions of power, from people whose only defense was weapons of bronze, to people who wielded iron. The impact must have been as shattering as that of the first use of Greek fire in the seventh century A.D., of gunpowder in the Middle Ages, or the atomic bomb today. Still, the older civilization did not disappear. It was, rather, absorbed. War and confusion produce a mingling of peoples and cultures. In Greece one culture grew out of another. The Minoans and the Mycenæans merged into the tradition of the Dorian invaders and became one in the great legend of the classic Greek people. The Dorian invasions ended around 1,000 B.C.

From then on, for about five hundred years, populations were probably more stable, and Greece was composed largely of two peoples: the Ionians and the Dorians. The Ionians were settled in the central Aegean regions, the Cycladic Islands and the narrow strip of Asia Minor coast. The Dorians occupied most of the Peloponnesus, Crete, and adjacent islands, and the southern corner of Asia Minor. Greece was emerging from dim antiquity into the light of recorded history.

Chapter Six

CITY=STATES AND COLONIES

(1,000-479 B.C.)

OUR KNOWLEDGE of the period between 1,000 and 800 B.C. is vague. Compared to the progress and splendor of earlier times, one might call this era the Dark Age of Greece. We do know that these years saw the genesis of a new chapter in civilization. The Aegean people had begun creating a society in which the individual was free to develop his political, intellectual, and æsthetic capacity. Instead of large groups of people, each distinguished by dialect and tribal customs, a number of cities, each with its own life and government began to develop. Small mountain plateaus and secluded valleys, inlets and coastal strips with population centers and natural barriers against outsiders, were now independent communities, to which the Greek people gave the name *polis*, which we translate literally as "city," but which implied an independent political organization better expressed as "city-state." Even small Aegean islands formed city-states of their own. Aristotle, the fourth-century philosopher, counted 157 on the mainland; and, though they used the same language, they often fought and more often quarreled.

Inhabitants of these cities called themselves "freemen," i.e. members of cities governed by a bill of rights, by laws or a constitution. The theory of individual rights springs from these early communities, which offered unrivaled opportunities to all the people for the discussion of public problems, and permitted the will of the majority to prevail.

The political and religious center and the place of assembly was a local strongpoint, a defensible hilltop. This usually is the beginning of the town. It was self-protected and self-sufficient at first. The people were scattered working all about. In time of war all came into the fortified acropolis. Though small, a city-state could extend its citizenship to neighboring communities. Often a group of states combined in a league and allied themselves for frontier security. In time of war they fought together as one. In time of peace they met to worship, hold games, festivals, and fairs.

In several parts of Greece there were sacred places called oracles where the gods made their will known to men. The most famous was the oracle of Apollo at Delphi, and here great festivals were held every two years to which men thronged from all parts of the ancient world. Anyone could consult the oracle, and anyone could join in the athletic games and in worship at the shrine. To Delphi, representatives from all parts of Greece came to discuss mutual problems and to insure peace and justice. This was called the Amphictyonic Council. It was really the first UNO.

Of all the city-states, two stand apart: Athens and Sparta. Athens, capital of all the Ionian Greeks, was the chief center of culture, and was typical of nearly all other cities except Sparta. Athens was open to all, a free and noble state, governed by the will of the people. But Sparta was a city closed to all except those of pure Dorian blood, and was bound by strict and unchanging laws. It was governed by a few men, called oligarchs, who ruled by force and fear.

Hemmed in and confined, Sparta lies twenty-five miles inland from the south coast of Peloponnesus, in the plain of Laconia. Mount Taygetus stretches along the whole western side of that plain.

Sparta is of great antiquity. Long before the Dorians conquered the older inhabitants, about 1,000 B.C., and made Sparta their capital, there was a school of sculpture here influenced by Cretan teachers. The Temple of Artemis is thought to be one of the oldest temples in Greece. Artists and craftsmen worked in bronze, clay and stone; poets and thinkers were welcome, and there was some ease and luxury.

In 730 B.C., the Spartans appropriated the nearby fertile plain of Messenia, but soon after, the Messenians sought help from neighboring states, revolted, and not only gained their freedom but defeated Sparta. Then arose the poet-statesman Tyrtæus, to inspire and guide the Spartans to victory again. The result of this second conquest altered their outlook on life. The Messenians, who had fought bravely and stubbornly for their freedom, were reduced to serfdom and were called Helots. They were allotted portions of land and were obliged to live and work there, paying their masters a fixed amount of produce. They were not exactly slaves, for they could not be sold. The Helots soon outnumbered the Spartans twenty to one, and became a constant threat. It was necessary to keep a kind of secret police moving among the Helot class, punishing or putting to death those suspected of plotting revolt. The Spartans knew quite well that this cruel practice was not enough to hold down freedom-loving people; they themselves must be ready to protect and defend their state at all times.

Conservatism and simplicity was the breath of Spartan life. Their laws, ideals and institutions were unlike those of other city-states. They came to believe that a wise lawgiver named Lycurgus had made the laws and arranged everything for them so there was no need to change anything. Lycurgus had gone to consult the oracle at Delphi on the wisdom of his laws. He was told that Sparta would grow strong and prosper so long as she kept his laws. So because he loved Sparta, and he had made the Spartans swear to keep his laws until he returned, he went away altogether and was never again seen by anyone. The story may not be true, but Sparta did keep his laws, rules, and regulations, and did not change them in the longest time in history. She became the strongest military land power in Greece.

Spartan society was divided into three classes: the sovereign *Lacedæmonians* (selectmen) on top; the *Perioikoi* (neighbors) who enjoyed civil but not political privileges and were free to support themselves by manufacture and trade, and at the bottom the Helots or community serfs.

Sparta was a police state; all citizens were in the army. The individual existed for the ideal and the good of the state. Physical fitness and aptitude for war were stressed. No smooth or elegant speech or writing was allowed. Family life was severely limited. Babies adjudged weak were done away with; boys lived with their mother until they were seven; from seven to twenty they were trained by the state and received the appropriate kind of military instruction and exercise. They also learned reading, writing, music and some arithmetic, and read passages from Homer and other poets. The hardest period in boys' lives was from eighteen to twenty when they were undergoing special training in warfare. But when this was finished, they themselves became instructors. Now they were allowed to marry, but not to live at home. Thirteen years of hard training, wrestling, running and quoit-throwing, made them stronge, agile, hardy and fearless, fit and ready for service in the field.

At the age of thirty, the Spartan became a full citizen, privileged to attend the Assembly and fill public office. He was allowed to live at home, but was still in the army and had his main meals in barracks, each man supplying his own share of barley meal, cheese, olives, figs or almonds, and money to buy fish or meat. Fifteen men shared a table, and fourteen voted to admit any new member. All dressed alike in a purple garment, and were close comrades in war and in peace.

A similar training existed for girls, but only until marriage. They were trained in mind and body to become mothers of brave and fearless men. They shared athletic exercises like the boys, and were given a careful physical training. They had games of their own too, the girls wearing so little that even Greeks from other cities were shocked. But temperance, virtue and simplicity were the cornerstone of Spartan society. Spartan women lived at home; and some acquired much property, living in moderate ease. But they were brave as their men, whom they ever urged to deeds of valor. When a Spartan mother handed the shield to her son going forth to battle she would lastly remind him in these famous words: *e tan e epi tas,* which means "Come back (victorious) with your shield, or (dead) upon it."

Though it seems cruel in some aspects and brutal in others, Spartan life was never superficial, and never vulgar or barren. The arts and sciences are the achievement of ideal and peace-loving states. Sparta did not create outward things of the spirit; she did create men.

Sparta had two kings at the same time. At home they were over-shadowed by the all-powerful Ephors or Overseers, five annual magistrates chosen by ballot. But a Spartan army abroad was always headed by one of the kings, who then had absolute power. There was also a Council composed of twenty-eight Elders past the age of sixty, who helped the Ephors in the management of public affairs, and considered measures to be brought before the Assembly or the whole citizen body. But the Assembly could not debate, and its decisions were carried not by voting but by shouting. The loudest shout won. It was a type of government which abolished nothing old and developed nothing new.

Sparta conquered first Laconia, then Messenia, reduced the people to serfdom and held them by fear. Athens unified all of Attica (a thousand square miles) by mutual consent, and peaceably brought it under her protection as part of one city-state. All inhabitants, class by class, were soon included in the citizenship of Athens. Many wealthier people came to live in the capital, but most people remained in their villages. Yet all were equally Athenians. This was most fortunate. Athens, surrounded by citizens and friends, was free to grow, to work and prosper.

The rulers of Athens were nine *archons,* chosen from certain noble families by the Assembly of all citizens who possessed property. Society was divided into classes according to wealth. All classes, except the lowest, voted in the Assembly when the archons were elected and sworn to rule according to the laws. Soon enough, the lowest class demanded a share in the government, and for the next one hundred and fifty years or so, changes were made from time to time, until all the people shared, leading Athens toward true democracy.

The first archon to draw a written code of laws for Athens "so that all the people can be governed alike" was Dracon, about 620 B.C., who is as shadowy as Lycurgus, the Spartan. One fact seems clear and that is the severity of his laws. People said that they were "written with blood and not with ink," nearly every offense no matter how small carrying a death penalty!

In 594 B.C. Athens elected Solon, a rich nobleman, as archon for the year. He is the first clearly recorded figure in Greek history. Being a merchant, he had traveled widely, and had observed the governments of other cities. He now resolved to help Athens. This was a time of oppression and unrest. In Attica there were many small farmers who were so poor that they borrowed money at high interest, on the security of their farms. These mortgaged lands were marked by "mortgage pillars" or boundary stones which stood there unmoved until the debt was paid. They had to pay more than half of their produce to the creditor. Sometimes people who had no land pledged themselves and their families instead, and if the debt was unpaid upon maturity, they became slaves who could be sold at home or abroad.

Solon is the first man in history to effect land reforms. He proclaimed the abolition of all securities on land and on persons, freed the slaves, and forbade people to sell themselves. Land debts thus incurred in the old fashion were canceled. This ordinance saved Athens from having Helots all around her.

Solon tried to make Athens the commercial and cultural center of Greece. First he declared Athens an open city and welcomed foreigners, especially artists and craftsmen. To make the Athenians public spirited, he gave to all the right to vote at the Assembly. Law courts were set up with citizens as jury. He then revised, and insisted upon, an accurate system of weights, measures and money. He instituted relief agencies for the poor, the old, the homeless. His many reforms freed, for the first time, the individual from strict ties of clan, family and religion. Solon's laws were written on wooden tablets and were placed where all could read them. Every citizen took an oath to obey them. Now a very bright flame shone on the acropolis, in a world of darkness. Even though Solon did not create full democracy, he did inaugurate a new chapter in the story of mankind.

Unfortunately, Solon's laws did not please all the people. Presently they were lined up in three parties; men of the hills, of the plains, and the shores. Leader of the hillmen was an ambitious noble, Peisistratos, who seized the Acropolis in 560 B.C. and imposed himself on the people. Because of the way he had usurped power, he was called "tyrant." That word has many meanings; it means a despotic ruler who governs without the consent of all the people; it also means a man who rules alone as he pleases without check or control. Many Greek cities at one time or another were ruled by tyrants, some of whom were good and wise men. A good tyrant was Peisistratos, who really cared for the welfare of the people. He knew well the inbred spirit of freedom in the Athenian, so he respected popular rights and worked to make Athens beautiful and powerful. The main entrance to the Acropolis, the Propylæa, was built and adorned with statues; engineers brought water in aqueducts from the hills into the market place. The famous Gymnasium and the Academy of Athens were built in Peisistratos' time. They played a most important part in the future life of the city.

Country life, agriculture and trade were encouraged. All over the Attic plain, the olive and the vine were cultivated and soon became an important source of revenue. Athenian settlements now reached to the Hellespont, and Athenian ships sailed the Aegean to and from Piræus. Athens under Peisistratos was rich, respected; the most important state in Greece. He died in 527 B.C.

About 508 B.C. a noble named Kleisthenes became ruler and proved himself a great statesman and democrat. He added something to Solon's and Peisistratos' work which made Athens the first true democracy in the world. He feared and disliked tyranny as a form of government, and to discourage it, he instituted the right of ostracism by popular demand. Once a year the people of Athens voted on potsherds called *ostrakon* against any individual judged dangerous to the state. The greatest danger were the wealthy nobles who somehow managed to find their way to the top of the government. To reduce this danger he abolished the four classes, each held together by kinship or religion. Kleisthenes divided the people into ten townships called *demoi*. Membership in the township was based on residence, instead of kinship or religion. Grouped this way, everyone, regardless of rank or class, rich or poor, had exactly the same rights and duties. Every ordinary citizen had a share; and each knew that he could rise to a high place in the service of his state. Opportunities for education and development were immense. Athens was a state of free citizens, the model state for the Greek world, for the entire world. Instead of remaining closed, fixed, and confined, Athens was free to advance. It did become the most wonderful city of the ancient world.

Recorded history properly begins with the first Olympic games in 776 B.C. Thereafter the events of each four-year period between the Games were noted and dated.

Early in the seventh century B.C. the Ionians introduced coinage from Lydia, a friendly neighboring country, rich in natural resources. The custom quickly passed to the Greek mainland. The world was never the same again. Greek traders brought coinage to the remotest corners of the known world, and coinage made the exchange of goods much easier. In time every city-state claimed the right to strike its own coinage. As a result, coins from hundreds of different mints came into circulation. Some were of exquisite design. The government which issued coins of precious metals, such as gold or silver, stood as guarantor of the value of its coins.

A most important factor in the cultural development of the Greeks was the alphabet, which was adapted from the Phœnician early in the ninth century B.C. By the fourth century B.C. the many Greek dialects and alphabets had given way to the Ionic, which soon was the language of nearly all Greek people. Papyrus was brought in from Egypt, and the art of writing came into general use. With it, of course, came a rapid increase in exchange of ideas, stimulating the growth of science and philosophy; bringing about a general awakening. Great changes came over art and literature. Poetry developed during this period, to reach its full flower in the Golden Age.

A new movement was afoot now, a four-way movement of colonization. Over-population was the chief cause, though to an extent also political unrest, wars, and discontent among the landless workers. The Greeks built wonderful seaworthy vessels and sailed the then known world. They were always voyaging and going places; they loved travel and sight-seeing. They regarded the sea as more important than

The Winged Victory of Samothrace, now in the Louvre, Paris

The Theatre at Delphi

The Parthenon at Athens

A typical peasant home of the North

Street scene in Northern Greece

Market scene in Northern Greece

A Dock laborer of Crete

The Island of Kalymnos

The common beast of burden in Greece

Goats are almost everywhere in Greece

A Greek village school

The Harbor at Piræus

A view of Crete

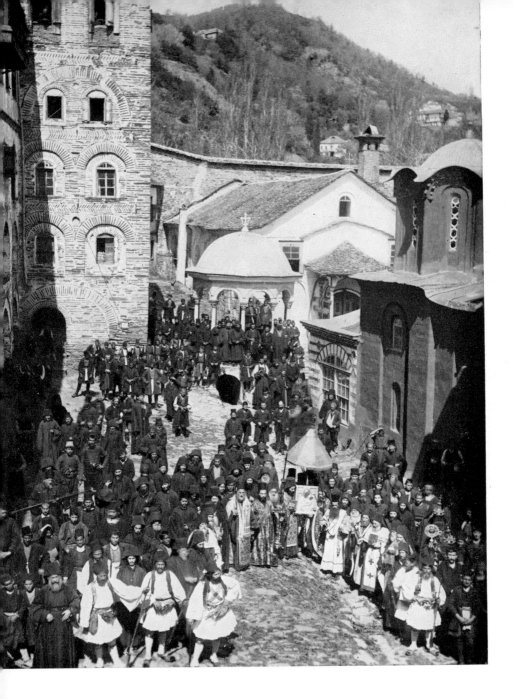

Holiday scene in a Greek monastery

The Cupbearer fresco at Knossos, Crete

Detail of the fresco

V. Papaioannou—Courtesy Arts, Inc.

Dodecanesian sponge-fishing fleet. In the upper picture
men are cleaning the sponges.

the land; the navy superior to the army. From the earliest times they had two kinds of boats: merchant ships, built and owned by individual citizens, and warships owned by the different states. The most common boat was the so-called *penteconter,* a ship of burden with fifty oars. They also built a small boat for twenty oars, for plying the nearby islands and fishing, sponge-fishing along the Aegean coasts. This boat, painted in bright Homeric designs, remains to this day a common sight in the Aegean. The most famous of all Greek vessels were the *triremes,* the galley-type battleships. A trireme had usually as many as two hundred rowers with three banks of oars on each side, and a three-pronged bronze beak for ramming enemy ships. It carried a single large mast and sail. A jigger mast was used for maneuvering.

Colonists carried with them the sacred fire from the town-hall of the mother-city, to be kept burning on the public hearth of their new home. In these and many other ways they kept the ties of kinship. Each colony was self-governing; the ties were purely cultural and sentimental. But even remote colonists always considered themselves a real part of Hellas, the motherland.

On the southern coast of Gaul the Phocians established Massilia (Marseilles), which became the chief center of trade in the west; other settlements were made in Spain and on most of the Mediterranean islands. The Greeks introduced the olive and the vine; they also brought in Ionian laws and the cult of Artemis, whose temple rose in every city. About the middle of the seventh century, people from Chalcis founded a colony near present-day Naples. From these colonists the Greek alphabet and the art of writing were adopted by the Romans, and were handed on, with a slight change to general European use. From these same people they also took the cult of Apollo.

About 730 B.C. Archias, a Corinthian who had colonized Corcyra (Corfu) on the west coast of Greece, went on to Sicily and founded Syracuse. It shortly became the most populous and best fortified city in Europe. The Spartans founded Messina and Agrigentum, from which they exchanged wine and oil for silver in the marts of Carthage, the most famous of all Phœnician cities. Another Spartan colony was

Tarentum in the instep of Italy, with an excellent harbor. So many Greek people lived in southern Italy that it was called Magna Græcia.

The Greek people were now scattered all around the rim of the Mediterranean. And as they expanded farther west they found themselves opposed by the Carthaginians, the Phœnicians and the Etruscans. Carthage especially was another great colonizing state and sought power in southern Italy and Sicily. An eventual struggle was impending.

A more serious threat at this time lay in the east, where older and more powerful empires arose to challenge Greece's eastward expansion.

In 550 B.C. a great country in western Asia was Lydia. Sardis was its capital and Crœsus its king. It included the many prosperous Greek cities of Ionia, which Crœsus had conquered. He was a wise benevolent, friendly man, and fabulously wealthy. The Lydian people were friendly and like the Greeks in many ways, though much more predominantly Asiatic. But Lydia was invaded and conquered by Cyrus of Persia. Cyrus became master of all Asia Minor, which was made part of the Persian Empire. After his death he was succeeded by his son Cambyses, who reigned for seven years and was succeeded by a relative, Darius.

Darius was an able administrator, a cautious military strategist, and a great organizer. He linked his empire together with many roads, of which the biggest ran 1,500 miles from Susa, his capital, to Sardis in Lydia, his headquarters in the west. His gigantic empire now included all the east-Mediterranean regions and extended far into central Asia. The whole world was slowly being brought within its grasp. Darius was master of millions of enslaved peoples. In Greece, hundreds of self-governing city-states vied with one another in every way, Athens and Sparta the chief contestants. Athens' navy had roused the jealousy of Sparta and of Corinth. But the Persian menace, which had already absorbed the Ionian cities, and was drawing nearer and nearer, united Athens and Sparta for a time.

Under Darius, the Greek cities of Ionia were allowed their religion, laws and customs. Each had its local government and managed its own affairs, but at its head was a *satrap* or petty despot appointed by the Persian king, and set there to see that due tribute was paid and that the citizens were loyal and served his army and navy when required. This form of government, much loved by the others, was utterly detested by the freedom-loving Ionian Greeks. In 499 B.C. they rebelled.

The uprising started at Miletus. One after another, other cities fired by the bright thought of gaining freedom, drove out their masters. Mother cities were now asked to send help. Sparta refused, but Athens sent twenty ships, and little Eretria in Eubœa sent five, which helped to attack Sardis, the important Persian headquarters in the northwest. They had almost taken the city, except the citadel, when a house thatched with reeds and straw caught fire accidentally, and set the whole city in flames. The siege was abandoned and the Athenians and Eretrians sailed home, but Sardis was left in ashes. Herodotus tells how Darius reacted on hearing the news:

"The Ionians he knew; they would be taken care of; they could never hope to escape punishment, but who, he wanted to know, were the Athenians? . . . When he was told, Darius asked for his bow, laid an arrow on it, and shooting it into the sky, called on Ormuzd, the greatest Persian god, to grant him vengeance. Then he instructed one of his servants to say to him three times each day, 'Master remember the Athenians.' "

Darius succeeded in conquering the rebellious Ionian cities in four years. He punished Miletus severely; all men were killed, women and children sent to Susa as slaves, and the city erased. The news of the fate of Miletus terrified the Greek world. Athens knew that her turn would come next.

In Athens now a great man was elected Archon for the year 493-492 B.C. He was Themistocles, who advocated total war for the defense of the state, and who, better than any one else, understood the importance of building a fleet, large enough to gain supremacy of the sea. He made this his major task. All parties to the Athenian democracy rallied to his support. At this time an able general returned to

Athens. Miltiades had served under Darius and knew his war tactics. He was elected to the board of generals. The Ionian revolt, costly as it was, had given the Greek people time to prepare, think and consolidate. There was not much time. Darius with his Persians was already on the march westward.

To conquer Greece, the Persians sent one small and two big expeditions. The first attempt to invade Greece was a failure, for a storm shattered nearly two hundred of the ships under Mardonius, Darius' son-in-law, in an attempt to round Mount Athos.

Two years later, Darius was ready to try again. First he sent heralds through the Greek cities and islands to demand "earth and water" as tokens of submission. Some islands and a few cities did give earth and water. Athens and Sparta refused.

Six hundred Persian ships bearing cavalry and infantry moved westward across the Aegean to Eretria, which had shared in the Ionian revolt. After a six-day siege, traitors opened the gates to the enemy, who sacked the city, burned the temples, and sent the people slaves to Darius. Then the fleet moved on to Marathon, on the east coast of Attica, twenty miles from Athens. Athens sent to Sparta a herald, the swiftest runner, one Pheidippides, who ran the 140 miles in 48 hours, and delivered this urgent appeal: "Lacedæmonians, the Athenians entreat you. Do not stand by idly waiting, while a most ancient city is about to fall into bondage to barbarians." But the Spartans were celebrating a religious festival, whose sacred laws forbade them to march until the moon was full. "We will come as soon after that as we can" the herald was told. Great events do not wait on the moon. The Persian fleet was already in the bay of Marathon. Athens was unwalled and without natural defenses.

It was a mellow summer noon in 490 B.C. Eleven Greek generals met in council on a hillside just above the plain of Marathon, which overlooks the sea. Callimachos was the commander-in-chief. This was the question: Should ten thousand liberty-loving people give battle to one hundred thousand of Darius' "invincibles" encamped on the plain below? For truly now the fate of Athens, of all Greece, of all Europe, was in the balance.

"Yes, a thousand times yes!" urged Miltiades. Other generals wavered.

Except for one thousand warriors from Bœotia, the nine thousand Athenians alone faced the Persian invaders. And they were resolute. They made ready; they took their position on the plain near the sea in a wide-stretched line. Again Callimachos held a council; the generals were divided, five for action, five for delay. Again Miltiades urged a bold stroke and the commander-in-chief agreed. Miltiades drew up his line to attack the enemy, nearly the same length as the Persian line, but while the Persian line was strong at the center and the wings entrusted to inferior troops, the Greek line was strong on the wings and only a few lines deep in the long thin center.

The signal for the attack was given and the Greek line advanced at a run. The Persians thought them mad the way they rushed forward shouting; they joined battle and easily broke through the thin Greek center and rushed on in pursuit. But carefully now the Athenian wings wheeled round, closing in behind, and shutting off the enemy from their ships; they routed the victorious Persian center and cut it down. Many fell on the spot, others fled to their ships pursued by the Athenians, who engaged them in a hand-to-hand battle, capturing seven ships. The Persian defeat was complete. The fleet sailed round the coast to within sight of Athens, and went on to Asia. After the full moon, two thousand Spartans came to Athens and went on to Marathon to see the battlefield. Praising the Athenians for their heroic stand, they returned to Sparta. Among the Athenians in the fight was Aeschylus and his brother. The brother was killed but Aeschylus came back to Athens and wrote three great tragedies called the Orestes-trilogy. They are: *Agamemnon, The Libation Bearers,* and *The Furies.*

Even though not crushing, the Persian defeat at Marathon shook the prestige of the Great King and encouraged rebellion throughout his empire. Now the conquest of Greece was one of practical necessity as well as honor. Darius himself would lead the final expedition, by land and sea against all Greece. Fortunately a revolt in Egypt kept the Persians busy for ten years. And these ten years decided the future of Athens. It so happened that in the mines of Sunion a very rich vein of silver was struck. Some people proposed that the money should be distributed in a kind of dividend among the citizens. But Themistocles persuaded the Athenians to spend it on a fleet, for he was sure that the Persian danger would come again.

The fleet was built, just in time. Darius died. Xerxes, his successor, was a weak and vain man. From his father he had apparently inherited only the desire for a terrible vengeance on the Athenians. He would overwhelm Greece with sheer numbers. Nothing could stop him from fulfilling his father's one wish to avenge the Persian defeat. He prepared for war on a vast scale. He gathered together a fleet and an army drawn from the whole strength of the forty-six nations comprising his empire. Along the route of invasion from Asia to the Hellespont great depots of provisions were established; a canal was dug across the stormswept isthmus of Mount Athos, where twelve years before his father's ships had been wrecked. Engineers built a bridge of boats across the Hellespont for the safe crossing of his army. Finally, all the forces were collected at Sardis. Here Xerxes received the news that the bridge was destroyed by a storm. Herodotus says that Xerxes in his rage ordered the engineers beheaded and the sea cursed and lashed with a scourge three hundred times! He then had a new bridge made of boats, surmounted by thick strong ropes and covered with planks and hedged on both sides so that the animals would not be frightened by the roaring waters.

Meanwhile in Greece a congress of deputies from all the cities was held at Corinth. Great was the danger; Xerxes was expected to start the invasion in early spring. He must be met, but where, how, by whom?

Athens and Sparta were united at this crucial moment; a feeling of common nationality for a struggle against a common enemy was now apparent among all the Greek states for the first time. Themistocles conferred the chief command of both land and sea on Sparta and drew a plan: the combined Greek fleet of about three hundred triremes would take its station at Artemision off northern Euboea, to meet the Persian fleet, while Leonidas, the Spartan commander, would proceed to defend the pass of Thermopylæ. Sparta with a well trained army was ready for her full share of the war on land.

Not trusting the sea, Xerxes decided to march his armies around the northern coast of Greece. The long story of the two-year war is most vividly recounted by Herodotus. It was the year 480 B.C., and when all was ready Xerxes set out from Sardis, gathering troops as he came from all the peoples beyond the Aegean.

When the army arrived at the Hellespont, before crossing, a halt was made for the king to review his forces. Seated on a lofty throne of white marble, Xerxes watched his army all around him filling shores and plains, and his armada so crowded and vast it hid the sea on which it rode. At sunrise the next morning, with his face turned to the sun, Xerxes from his throne overlooking the strait poured libation into the sea from a golden cup, and prayed that nothing should stop him from punishing Greece. Now the long lingering line began to move across the bridge, marching west into the plain of Thrace. Xerxes made a stop to count his troops. Herodotus says they were so many, far too many to be numbered one by one, that batches of ten thousand were crowded into a space which just held them. This space was filled and cleared 170 times.

Marching west through Macedonia, the Persians turned southward, scorching the earth, scourging, conquering, drinking the rivers dry as they advanced. Ahead of the army went Persian heralds calling on all cities, demanding "earth and water." Town after town gave its handful of earth and water, town after town gave up its freedom. One by one the northern defenses went down. The invaders swarmed on until they came to the place called Thermopylæ (Hot Gates), a narrow pass between sea and mountains, an actual gateway to Greece. This they found blocked and guarded by Leonidas and three hundred Spartans, together with about five thousand Peloponnesians, Bœotians and Phocians.

Xerxes pitched his camp in the region called Malis; the hostile camps lay only three miles apart, and Xerxes simply waited, expecting the Greeks to withdraw in terror as his vast armies accumulated. For four days his myriads of troops pressed into the narrow land. The Greeks made no move. His spies reported that the Spartans were in the front of the Greek line, and did not seem in the least troubled or dismayed; on the contrary, they were busy at their games, exercising, exhibiting themselves in front of their positions, combing their long black hair, as they always did before going into battle. Xerxes was amazed and ordered his troops to attack, capture and bring them alive before him. He himself sat on his throne and watched. Two days he sat and saw his Immortals driven back; the Greeks holding the pass; three times the astounded king leaped from his throne in rage. Then a certain Ephialtes appeared and betrayed to the Persians a secret by-path over Mount Kallindromon. In the night word came to Leonidas that his forces were being cut off from behind. At daybreak he dismissed his allies, save for a thousand Phocians, seven hundred Thespians; the Thebans, and three hundred Spartans. As they waited for the attack, hemmed in on both sides by great numbers, they were warned that there was no retreat and no escape once the Persians closed in, and they were so numerous that when they shot their arrows they hid the sun and blotted out the sky. "Good," was their reply, "we'll be fighting in the shade!"

The Persians did close in, officers flogging their men forward, and were met by free and fearless men fighting for freedom. Leonidas was slain. Withdrawing, the Spartans carried him on their shoulders to a small hillock which rose above the pass. Here they stood and battled bravely until, one by one, all but two of the Spartans perished defending the pass. Their glorious devotion to country and duty forms one of the brightest pages of all history.

Unopposed, the Persians marched toward Athens through Bœotia, laying waste the country as they advanced. Town after town sent earth and water. Athens was in terror and despair. The oracle at Delphi had said to the Athenian envoys: "Trust the wooden walls, and fly to the ends of the earth." Still, the Athenians did not submit. Even when Sparta, who was as determined as Athens to resist, proposed to withdraw her troops and defend only Peloponnesus, refusing at first to consider any other plan, Athens stood firm, though her cause seemed hopeless. Athens stood firm even when Xerxes' ambassador came and offered the most generous terms, everything they wanted—everything except freedom. "Tell Xerxes," was their answer, "as long as the sun moves on its orbit in its present course the Athenians will never come to terms with Xerxes."

The oracle at Delphi had spoken again: "Zeus sends a wooden wall to Pallas Athena, which will save and preserve you and your children." And there was a great dispute as to the meaning of the message; some thought it meant the ships; others thought it meant the wooden palisade around the Acropolis. But now Themistocles returned to Athens and prevailed. He said the ships were the wooden wall of the oracle, and persuaded the people to withdraw to the nearby island of Salamis, which would provide a secure refuge as long as the fleet held out.

The Greek fleet, well equipped and resolutely manned, was numerically inferior to the Persian. It lay between the invader and the future of Athens, of all the civilized world.

The Persians entered Athens and found it empty, except for a few stalwarts who had sought refuge in the wooden palisade. Flaming arrows were shot against them and soon all Athens was in flames. Xerxes sent the news to Susa: "Sardis is avenged!" From their ships in nearby Salamis, the Athenians could see the flames of their burning temples and houses. Their scouts reported that the Persian fleet was at anchor in the nearby bay of Phaleron.

Now comes one of the most momentous debates in history. The Peloponnesian land forces were at the Isthmus, where a wall was hurriedly built across it to protect them, and most of the sea captains were in favor of moving all the allied Greek fleet back there from Salamis, afraid that it might be blockaded and bottled up by the more numerous Persian ships. Themistocles was much disturbed, for he knew that the Greek ships, nearly two-third of them Athenian, could fight with some hope against the enemy fleet in narrow waters where the enemy would not be able to maneuver freely and where the Persian numbers would not count so heavily. But, more important, he knew and feared that it would mean the ruin of the Athenian refugees who would be left behind to slavery or massacre. He saw that the narrow waters inside Salamis would give the allied Greek fleet the best chance of victory, while at the Isthmus the fleet would not hold together and would most certainly be defeated. So, he urgently persuaded Eurybiades, the Spartan commander-in-chief, to call all the captains and reopen the debate. He agreed, and before the question was formally put before the war council, Themistocles began to speak, urging his case for fighting in the narrows of Salamis. He was interrupted again and again, but he went on. Suddenly Eurybiades, infuriated, raised his cane to strike. Themistocles cried: "First listen to me; then you can strike me!" and warned him that unless he agreed to stay and fight at Salamis the Athenians would sail away in their ships and refound their life in Italy. Eurybiades agreed to stay.

The next thing was to induce Xerxes to battle where he wanted him to, in the narrows. This was perfectly simple to Themistocles. He contrived to send a friendly message which would be sure to fall into the Persians' hands indicating that they should act quickly because the Greek fleet was on the point of slipping away, that the Greeks would retreat during the night, by the western exit of the bay, and if the Persians would block up this exit, they would bottle up the whole Greek fleet.

Xerxes walked into this trap. Confident in the size of his fleet, and impatient for victory, he sent one detachment to the western exit; the rest of the fleet was crowded into the narrow waters between the mainland and the narrow peninsula of Salamis. The Persian fleet was split in two by the tiny island Psyttalea. Xerxes himself, surrounded by spearmen sat on his throne on a hill overlooking the eastern strait, to watch the battle. His scribes were there too, ready to record the great victory. To the west, unseen, were countless other people waiting, whose fate hung on the outcome of this battle; they were the many thousand Athenian fugitives praying that they might be saved.

It was dawn. The Persian fleet in force now moved forward to bottle up the Greeks, who advanced to meet them. The great number of Persian galleys crowding the narrowing straits of Salamis, lacking enough room to deploy and move freely, were soon helplessly and hopelessly entangled together; thrown into confusion by their own great numbers; driven side to side and end to end. The Greek ships swooped down like hawks and rammed at their enemies before they had time to open out into the broader reaches of the bay. The Greeks boarded the Persian decks and set them on fire. The Persians were forced back upon themselves, only increasing the fatal congestion. Their great ships and weapons were useless; they had to resort to hand-to-hand fighting; while the Greeks could advance and as quickly move back for another thrust. The Bay swarmed with struggling figures, and at every slight advance the Greeks hurled fire into the enemy fleet. Before Xerxes' own eyes more than two hundred of his ships were sunk, others hopelessly aflame.

At sunset it was all over. The Greek people had gone into battle almost despairingly. Now they could not believe their own eyes. Though they held ready and fully expected another battle, the terrible menace was over. In the night the remnant of the Persian fleet fled to the Hellespont; Xerxes himself was homeward bound by the same land route he had come. He left his son-in-law, Mardonius, with a large army to winter in Thessaly. He, too, was beaten in a great battle at Platæa, in Bœotia (479 B.C.), this time by the magnificent steadiness of the Spartans. Mardonius was slain.

Xerxes made no further attempt to conquer Greece. Athens and Sparta in the last hour, had saved the Western world.

Chapter Seven

THE GOLDEN AGE

(479-362 B.C.)

THE AMAZING triumph over Persia moved the Greek people to a new sense of their national greatness. More than ever before they realized the meaning of liberty. Sparta's fame never stood higher. And Athens had thrown herself into the conflict with supreme courage, refusing to yield to almost certain destruction. She even had given up her city, in order to continue the fight for the rest of Greece. Her steadfastness won for her command of the sea. Persia was now on the defensive.

At about this time, the Greek people of southern Italy inflicted crushing defeats upon the Carthaginians and the Etruscans, who sought to plunder the Greek colonies there. The Greeks then became the dominant people in the Mediterranean world.

When the Athenians brought back their families to Attica, they found the country laid waste and Athens ruined and desolate. The people began to rebuild and to make a wall round the city. One had been started years before but was not even half finished.

Now the city would be well fortified with a bigger and stronger wall, in spite of Sparta's efforts to the contrary, for she sent envoys, demanding that it be stopped, as it would turn the city into a stronghold should the Persians invade Greece again and take Athens. Other cities sent warning too. But Themistocles knew the real reason, and sparring for time, put men, women and even children to work until the wall was completed. Traces of the haste with which the work was carried on may be seen to this day in the curious mixture of materials (stones, broken columns, anything they could lay hands on) brought to light in recent excavations. To ensure the permanent union of the town and its harbor, Themistocles began to fortify Piræus, as well. A massive wall inclosed the three harbors within its circuit; strong moles guarded the entrances, and the city and its port were connected by a way 200 yards wide and five miles long, between stone walls 15 feet thick.

But just when the Long Walls were being finished, Themistocles was banished. He was suspected of having treacherous dealings with the Persians, a charge which was never actually proved.

Athens found herself again, and regained her life and work. A new note of idealism was apparent; and a spirit of enterprise and adventure. The many maritime cities of Asia Minor and the islands were still for the most part under Persian rule, but now seeing Persia defeated in Greece, they all formed a union to throw off the hated yoke. They appealed to Sparta for aid and leadership, but always cautious and reluctant Sparta hung back. Athens came forward and accepted the role of leadership, throwing all her energy and resources into the crusade.

In 478 B.C. the island of Delos was made the headquarters of the Delian League, as the union was called, which in purpose was somewhat similar to the Atlantic Pact of our own times. The little island now became the center of religious worship of all the Ionian Greeks. Here the League council deliberated and stored its funds in the temple. All the states had equal vote, and a common fleet and treasure, and each member state contributed annually a fixed number of ships and men; or, if they preferred it, the equivalent in money. Athens had the greatest number, a fleet of 200 triremes.

The headquarters of the Delian League were moved to Athens, and the confederacy was converted into a league of states subject to herself, with its fleet as her power and under her command, and its big treasury at her disposal. Increase of wealth meant more leisure for her citizens, and more time to be devoted to civic duties. The time and occasion for great achievement had arrived—and with it the right man.

Pericles, the distinguished statesman, leader of the people, patron of the arts, in his own personality expressed the highest ideals of his age. Born an aristocrat, he fought for democracy. He guided the affairs of Athens for over thirty years. His predominance in the Assembly was almost undisputed from 461 until his death in 429 B.C. He reshaped the civic life of the state, even curtailing the sacred powers of the highest judicial court. The complexion of the Council, the Assembly, and the Law courts was altered. Finally he gave the people a new constitution, and carried a measure in the Assembly for payment of jurors and other civil workers, for he wanted every citizen to be able to take part in the government.

The first thing Pericles did was to call a congress of all Greek cities, and try to persuade them to join in a co-operative group and work together to restore the shrines and monuments destroyed in the wars, as a gratitude and thank-offering to the gods. When the other cities refused to work together, he alone proceeded in the rebuilding of Athens, for which he used the money in the treasury of the common fund of the Delian League now stored in the Acropolis. "We throw open our city to all," he told objectors, and proceeded to make Athens the most splendid city in Greece. He was a great believer in beauty. His home was the haunt of sculptors, poets and philosophers. The great master of the Attic School of sculpture was his friend Pheidias. To him Pericles entrusted supervision of the grandiose scheme he had adopted for rebuilding Athens.

Within twenty years the steep hill of the Acropolis was crowned by massive buildings and monuments honoring Athena. The temples were built of white marble and were painted in part with bright colors. They must have looked very noble in the sparkling Attic air, rising serenely against the setting of purple mountains and blue sea. On the hill towered the great figure of Athena Promachos, the goddess who fights in the forefront of battle, so high that the gilded crest of the helmet and twinkling spearpoint could be seen by sailors soon after rounding Cape Sunion, the southernmost point of Attica. On moonlit nights the statue was a kind of beacon light. Beyond it was one of the most renowned buildings of the world—the Parthenon. It was enclosed by a portico of Doric columns, 34 feet high, and the whole shrine was built of creamy white marble, and adorned with statues by Pheidias. His masterpiece was a gigantic figure of the goddess, which was placed in the interior of the Parthenon, and which represented for the Athenians the very embodiment of the goddess herself, standing ready to defend their city.

Just west of the Acropolis was the Pnyx, the open-air theatre-like space cut out of the rock of a hill, where the Athenian legislature met once a month. This Assembly, a mass-meeting of all native men, was the sole legislative body. Any citizen, any year, might find himself in any office of the government. It was not unusual to find a man an Athenian general in one campaign and a private soldier in the next, for generals and admirals were elected annually; re-election, however, was permissible and quite normal. "To rule and to be ruled in turn" was the basic concept of Athenian democracy.

If one approached the city from the west, he would first pass through the streets of craftsmen of all sorts, from metal workers, cobblers and ropemakers, fullers' shops, basket-weavers, to shield-and-spear makers, and skilled workers in gold and ivory. Each man ran his own business, often helped by apprentices. A craft or art was called *techne* from which our word "technical" is derived. Men of the same craft joined in guilds, held common religious rites and even lived in some separate quarter of the town.

The potters' quarter was known as Cerameicus or Street of Tombs. Pottery was a great industry in Greece through every period. All cities produced pottery for export; it found its way to all corners of the world; and there are no more priceless treasures in our museums than the Attic, Corinthian, or even Minoan vases. With the potter worked a well-known artist who decorated the vase, with scenes drawn from mythology or daily life, done in black and white on the reddish clay. Both were so proud of their work that they often signed it: "Epitimos made me," "Douris painted me," "Exekias drew me," or inscribed it, "hail and drink well" or *"is hygeian"* (to your health). And no two vases were alike.

There were many famous theatres in Greece and the theatre of

Dionysos at Athens was the cradle of dramatic art. In it were first performed the masterpieces of Greek tragedy. It was open to the sky, almost circular, with descending tiers of seats, cut out of the rock of the southern slope of the Acropolis. On each of the three days of the festival of Dionysos, at dawn, the people flocked to this theatre. The fifteen thousand seats were backless and narrow and hard. Some were carved from the rock or constructed of stone so people brought a cushion along with their day's provisions. The front tier was reserved for magistrates, archons, priests, and ambassadors from foreign states, and the very center seat of honor for the priest of Dionysos. From this theatre in Athens the people could look south across four or five miles of plain to the coast and the sea.

It was past noon when the performance was over. Then the audience would disperse, to return at dawn on the following two days for hearing other works. The festival was a contest for the best written and best produced plays. Tragedy was always followed by a comedy or a burlesque. At the close of the festival the verdict was given by judges chosen from the whole citizen body, so it reflected the public taste.

The father of Attic tragedy was Thespis (about 535 B.C.); hence people associated with the stage are sometimes called "Thespians." But the real inventor of the drama was Aeschylus (525-456 B.C.), who introduced a second actor, diminished the importance of the chorus and assigned the leading part to the dialogue. With such limited cast, he was able to create and produce *Prometheus Bound,* the first great drama. Aeschylus who fought with the infantry at Marathon, wrote in a grand and rugged style and composed seventy plays gaining the prize for dramatic excellence thirteen times. *Prometheus, Agamemnon, The Persians,* and *Choëphoræ* are some of his best known dramas.

The next great name is Sophocles (496-406 B.C.) who was a commander in one of the later wars, and who added a third actor and used some form of scene painting. He is serene, calm and more polished. Of his many plays only seven have survived, *Antigone* and *Oedipos Rex* perhaps the best known. Euripides (480-406 B.C.), the greatest of the tragic Greek poets, wrote ninety-two plays, seventeen of which have been preserved. His plays move quickly and are full of human interest, life and action. The tragedies of *Oedipos the King, Electra, The Trojan Women, The Bacchœ* and *Seven Against Thebes* are read in all languages, for they are very eloquent, though serious and profound.

There came another great writer, whose plays deal with man and his earthly playthings, the society in which he lives, works, toils and laughs. He was Aristophanes, writer of comedies. His many plays held up to ridicule and criticism outstanding men of the day, found fault with the government or dealt with important questions of peace and war. There is a mixture of beauty and coarseness, mellow wit and rough play in his comedies. They were usually performed in the afternoon, after the tragedies, and brought to a close the great Dionysian festivals.

From the earliest times of which we have any record the Greek people were passionately fond of athletic games. To them we owe a large measure of our interest in gymnastic sports. Athletics, derived from the Greek word *"Athlon"* (the contest itself, or a prize given in a contest), were part of the education of every Greek boy, and the life of every Greek man.

The rich kept horses and raced them, chiefly in harness. Enormous sums were spent on the training of teams and the maintenance of stables. Homer describes a chariot race in connection with the funeral games celebrated in honor of Patroclus, the friend of Achilles. Two- or four-horse team races were very common, and part of all national games. Though women were not allowed to compete in the games, and were excluded from watching them, we hear of chariot teams owned by them being driven in the races and winning prizes! We also hear of as many as forty entries in a single race. The charioteers were for the most part professionals, like our own jockeys; and as in races of our own time, the prize went to the owner or trainer.

As the cities grew, everywhere small training-grounds for boys, called *Palœstrai,* or wrestling-schools were built. But outside the city itself stood great open-to-the-sky gymnasia, usually placed near a stream and a grove of trees for shade and coolness in hot summer days, and surrounded by avenues of trees and colonnades. They were really public gathering halls for all men, who met there to practise physical culture and discuss their affairs.

Two mottoes best express the Greek spirit: "Nothing in excess," and "Moderation in all things." They loved the human form and believed in a sound mind in a sound body. This found expressions in all forms of everyday life and activity. Physical perfection was exemplified in festivals and public games, which further contributed to the cultivation of the sense of beauty. And there were many opportunities all over Greece for display of individual prowess, for competitions and races were part of the religious festivals. In addition to special festivals in honor of the gods of a single city, there were others which were attended by people from all over the Greek world. But most famous were the Olympic Games, supposedly founded by the hero, Heracles, which took place at Olympia in Elis, on the west coast of the Peloponnesus.

Every four years at the first full moon, heralds came to each city in Greece to invite free-born citizens to Olympia, to share in the festival to be held in late summer. Whether in Greece itself or as far as Egypt, the Black Sea, or Italy, the heralds were welcomed, and everywhere not only the athletes themselves prepared to start on their journey, but delegates chosen to represent their city in the ceremonies, since it would have been impossible for all citizens to go. The heralds proclaimed a Sacred Truce, and all war and fighting stopped so that the journeys to Olympia by land or sea routes should be safe. Larger states were usually represented by embassies of pomp and magnificence.

Olympia was a sacred place, like the Acropolis at Athens, or the Oracle at Delphi. Athletic contests were only part of the festival. All buildings for athletes and for the contests—the Stadion, the Palæstra, the Gymnasium, and the Hippodome—lay outside the sacred enclosure. Within the sacred space were many temples and altars, the marble temple of Zeus being the most magnificent. And in this temple was enshrined one of Pheidias' greatest works: the majestic statue of Olympian Zeus. People said "Either the God himself descended to show his form, or Pheidias himself ascended to heaven and beheld the God."

On the very first day on the great altar just outside the temple, judges, trainers and athletes offered sacrifices and took an oath that they would be fair in the contests. And again on the third day, a great procession of all the pilgrims, judges, priests, delegates and athletes made a solemn sacrifice at the altar of Zeus, and olive branches were plucked from the sacred tree for the wreaths which were the rewards for victory in the games. On the fifth day the victors themselves, crowned with these wreaths offered their own sacrifices to Zeus.

Greek people attached extraordinary value to the Olympic olive-branch. Its acquisition gave lifelong distinction to the winner. If an athlete had won three events in the games, his statue was permanently set up in Olympia itself. Victories in the games were celebrated in a way which was natural to an enthusiastic and artistic people; sculptors made statues, and poets wrote odes in their honor. But in addition to athletes, celebrated historians, poets, and philosophers read from their works, and orators addressed the audience at Olympia. Even Themistocles and later Plato and others were received with honor by the admiring multitude.

The state of the civilized world in the fifth century before Christ, was the world of Greece, of city-states ringing the eastern Mediterranean, and hundreds of colonies scattered from the Black Sea, along the Asia Minor coast south to Egypt and west to southern Italy. Other cultures existed outside this world, but they were either dead or dying. And in this compact little world, Athens, the great sea power, and Sparta, the great land power, with its allies close around her, waged the longest and bloodiest civil conflict in the ancient world. It lasted for about thirty years (432-404 B.C.), and involved and nearly destroyed the whole Greek world. This was the Peloponnesian War. An historian named Thucydides, who lived through it first as an Athenian general, then as a careful observer, recorded in minute detail the graph of disaster. When the war started Spartan arms were invincible, and Athenian seapower at its peak. The world of Greece was a whole civilization—a majestic one—and in both leading states, and through the smaller, the dream of a Panhellenic union—a United States of Greece—a strong and abiding confederation of all the states into one peaceful country, seemed to rule men's minds as never before. But then suddenly, except for brief intermissions, fighting went on in almost every part of Greece, all over the Aegean, in and around the Bosporus, in Bœotia, in Asia Minor, Italy and Sicily, around the coasts of Peloponnesus, in northwest Greece, and around both Athens and Sparta themselves. Why? What was the real cause of this terrible war? Power, Thucydides wrote, or its equivalent wealth, created the desire for more power, more wealth; greed for more of both, power and wealth, which no power and no possession satisfy, and which is in human nature and the cause of all wars. It was not a question of right or wrong, or a right power or wrong power. Power itself was the corruptor of men.

We have seen how in a quarter of a century, the confederacy of Delos developed into the Athenian Empire. This roused ill-feeling, fear and opposition in Sparta, and when in the course of trade rivalry Athens gained control of routes leading south to the Isthmus, and soon after took over the harbors formerly held by Corinth, Aegina, and other towns, they too, conceived an extreme hatred for Athens.

Sparta was also the leading state in Greece, and now she saw her position being threatened and her trade and influence in great danger, and the Greek cities, once free and independent, now "enslaved" as she thought, in the firm grip of Athens. Secretly she plotted and encouraged rebellion within the Delian League; she even came forward as the defender of Greek freedom, championing the complete independence of each city-state. But the League was one with the Athenian Empire. So Sparta herself gathered round her a group of mainland states and formed her own tightly-knit Peloponnesian League.

The hour was perilously late. Pericles was quick to realize the great danger to Greek peace; and called a conference. To all the states went deputations asking for an assembly at Athens. "But nothing was effected" Plutarch wrote laconically, "nor did the cities meet by their deputies, owing to the opposition of the Spartans." So deep was fear and mistrust now between the Greek states that the people, once free to act and speak for themselves, were afraid not only to work for, but even to think of, peace. No greater tragedy than this could ever befall a people. Pericles reconciled himself to the situation and prepared for war, for he knew so very well that liberty has always to be fought for, defended and re-won.

While the two leading powers watched and waited without striking directly at one another, the actual fighting began among the colonies. In 433 B.C., Corcyra, an island off the west coast of Greece, was suddenly torn by a local quarrel with her mother-city Corinth, a Spartan ally, and in the course of conflict turned to Athens for help. This affair was the spark that set on fire the whole Greek world, because when Athens did send help to Corcyra, Corinth appealed to Sparta. The Athenians no sooner won this struggle than a second similar battle broke out, this time over Potidæa. Again the Athenians won, routing a Corinthian army. Beaten and enraged Corinth conceived an extreme hate for Athens, who at the same time held the passes leading south to the Isthmus and had taken over the harbors and trade routes formerly held by herself. Corinth appealed to Sparta to declare war. A conference of all the allies was called at Sparta. In vain Archidamos the wise Spartan commander made a final plea: "Let us never be elated by the fatal hope of the war being quickly ended. Nay, I fear rather that we may leave it as a terrible legacy to our children."

After long discussions, the members of the Peloponnesian League voted for war. On the side of Sparta were almost all the members of her League, including Corinth and Megara and all of Bœotia except Platæa. Sparta had her own large army, trained and drilled to the utmost, the best in the world, which could almost surely win a victory in a pitched battle with any other state. On the side of Athens were a few allies, members of her League, and a large sum of money laid aside for war. Athens had no land army to match its enemy, but had her great navy. And Athens had a well fortified port which Sparta and her allies could never hope to take by assault.

The greatest land power and the greatest sea power in Greece faced each other in war; the stake was the leadership of Europe, the year was 431 B.C. and the time was in early summer when the grain was ripe. The pattern of war was set. The Spartan armies invaded Attica for the first time, destroying the grain and the orchards. On the advice of Pericles, the country people came into Athens. They were safe from the enemy, but their farms were left open to the Spartan armies, and were systematically devastated. The Spartans came to within six miles of the city. They destroyed the areas outside of Athens, in full view of the Athenians guarding the walls, and in a shrewd hope of rousing indignation to the point where unreasoning pressure of public opinion, once unleashed by crisis, can rage through a democracy and bring its ruin. If they could only madden the Athenian people enough to clamor for action, to force their leaders into the bold folly of meeting them on their own terms—a land battle. And indeed, watching from their walls, the enraged Athenians, especially the young men, cried for arms and leadership to rush out and put a stop to Spartan ravaging. They gathered in knots disputing hotly and denouncing Pericles for not leading them against the Spartans.

But Pericles saw the problem clearly. He knew that no land army could stand a chance in battle with the Spartans. He knew also that with the Athenian fleet commanding the seas, and providing the city with food, and guarding most of the empire, the soundest plan would be a slow and cautious war of attrition. This strategy demanded leadership, forbearance, steady nerves, and above all, time. And only these could save Athens. So, firmly he held the people back, and instead of a land battle dispatched one hundred triremes to harass the enemy's own towns along the coast of Peloponnesus. For many years the war was to be fought in this manner on both sides.

The Spartans exhausted their supplies and went home before winter set in. At the end of a year's fighting, a public funeral was held for those who had fallen. Their bones were brought to Athens, and were carried in a great procession of ten carriages, and there was one empty bier covered with a pall, in honor of the Unknown Soldiers whose bones were missing. The burial was followed by an oration which has come down as one of the finest tributes in history. This is Pericles' Funeral Oration, in which he spoke in glowing praise of Athens "the school of Hellas," the city of free men, lovers of beauty and wisdom, whose men of courage, when called to action went forth, fought and died for freedom, leaving an undying memory for all generations to come.

The next spring the Spartans again invaded Attica; the Athenian navy raided the coast towns around Sparta. But before the summer had ended, a far more deadly enemy had invaded Athens in the form of a terrible plague. It spread quickly in the crowded and unhealthy conditions and struck everywhere. People were seized without any apparent reason, with violent heats; the dead lay as they fell, one on top of another, while others hardly alive crowded every fountain, craving for a drink of water. Nearly a third of the people died of it. Humbly the Athenian people sought peace with Sparta in vain. In their misery and despair, they now turned against Pericles, unjustly laying the blame on him for their misfortune, fined him and suspended him from office.

Leaders arose who swayed the people by unprincipled oratory and pandered to their prejudices. Kleon is an example of the new kind of leadership. He was ruthless, clever, self-confident, and notorious for his vulgar and violent behavior on the platform of the Assembly. In 425 B.C. the Athenian navy in a dramatic battle seized a headland called Pylos, west of Sparta, and forced surrender of the Spartan garrison of 420 men, which Thucydides says, amazed all Greece. The Spartans were so depressed by this that they sent envoys to Athens with offers of peace and long friendship. But this did not suit Kleon and his war party. He demanded so much more that the Spartan envoys left in disgust. How different, indeed, would have been the story of Greece, if at this point wiser leaders and sensible men had ruled in Athens. But no, Kleon wanted war, and the fires of revolution and social warfare raged beyond control. Partisans of the two great protagonists lashed every state and every colony near and far into civil war.

There came at last a lull, after ten years of fighting, and after both Brasidas, the Spartan commander and Kleon himself were killed in battle. The peoples and armies were weary of the long fighting, so bloody and so inconclusive.

The last act of Greece's tragedy changes scene. We have seen how Greek colonies were founded and cities grew up all around the rim of the Mediterranean Basin. In the east, war was almost continuous, but in the west, comparative peace had brought increasing wealth to the colonies of Sicily and south Italy. By far the richest and strongest city now was Syracuse, a colony founded from Corinth. Her rulers lived in luxury, and their magnificent courts attracted many famous men, among them Aeschylus from Athens and Pindar from Thebes. The city was called the Athens of the West.

But for a long time, in her pride and power Syracuse made war herself or supported others to war on cities friendly to Athens. Through overbearing ways Syracuse made enemies who resented her cruel treatment and regretted their lost liberties. Even though four hundred miles away, Athens was on friendly terms with some of these cities, and was more than anxious over the growing power of Syracuse. Had the time come to check, or even break her power, which already was a threat to her grain supply?

Party politics, and struggle for leadership remained the main feature of Athenian democracy. And dominating the whole scene was the elegantly attired and oddly intriguing figure of Alcibiades. His strongest adversary was the peace-loving general Nicias, a moderate, religious, honest and respected man. But he lacked force and decision much needed at this most critical moment; and it fell to his lot to have to work with one his very opposite in character. Alcibiades was young, rich, handsome, and brilliant. He was surrounded by boosters and flatterers who finally convinced him that he was the man of the hour, the great commander, who would indeed surpass even Pericles himself. Not even the teachings of his great friend, Socrates, for whom he had real respect, could change his mind about himself. Many Athenians, dazzled by his eloquence, the splendor of his clothes, and his immense competence were ready to follow and support him in all his ambitious schemes. They could not see that he was working against their city and even against peace. He had formed in his mind the idea of a great campaign in the west. Italy, Carthage, the coasts of Africa could all be won and added to the Athenian Empire, under his own brilliant leadership. In 416 B.C. a quarrel arose between Segesta, the Athenian ally, and Selinus, supported by Syracuse. Segestan messengers came to Athens soliciting help. This was the chance Alcibiades was waiting for. For, though Sicily was far beyond the arena of war, could this great prize be brought to the Athenian side, it might decisively change the course of the whole struggle.

Alcibiades had his opportunity. He painted to the Assembly a glowing picture of a great empire in the west, and so influenced the people that they voted for an expedition, in the pretense of helping an ally. The critical opposition of Nicias, a sober leader who warned them not to undertake a war which did not directly concern them, was brushed aside and merrily forgotten.

Arriving in Sicily, Alcibiades and Nicias clashed on strategy, wasting provisions, discouraging their own men, and exciting contempt in the minds of the Sicilian Greeks. When at last Alcibiades' plan had been accepted, which called for a grand assault on Syracuse, the island's key city and Sparta's principal ally, Alcibiades himself had to return home. His enemies had taken advantage of his absence, charged him with sacrilege and induced the Assembly to vote for his recall. The fleet sailed on to Syracuse, an army landed and began to hem the city with a wall from south to north. The Syracusans were in despair, for they were unable to cut this with counter-walls, and the Athenian fleet was slowly moving into the Great Harbor.

But fortune soon turned against the Athenians. Many months were wasted deliberating and delaying until Nicias laid belated siege to the city. En route to Athens to face the charges, Alcibiades calculated that opinion had been aroused against him at home, and even people who had idolized him would now ask for his execution. He escaped ship and fled to Sparta, turned traitor and revealed the Athenian expedition's plans. A new Spartan army invaded Attica, devastating areas around Athens. Gylippos, an able Spartan commander, was dispatched with an army to Syracuse.

Gylippos' arrival changed the whole picture in the battle for Syracuse. He soon had the Athenians on the defensive. Under cover of night eighty Syracusan triremes moved out to meet the Athenian fleet. A land force captured three forts where most of the Athenian provisions were stored. The pincers slowly closed around the Athenians. They were soon cut off on the north and the south, and the Syracusans were in command of both sides of the entrance to the Great Harbor. At last, Nicias found his fleet pinned down by the enemy's counterblockade. He tried brashly to break through the trap. He was beaten at every turn and his 42,000 men were put to flight. With their ships lost, they started to retreat by land, cut and clawed fiercely by the enemy. Everything was destroyed and few returned home.

The bloody civil war was now on its twenty-fifth year. Great changes had come over Athens. Yet all the time the life of the Polis went on. The people continued their games and festivals as part of the life which they were fighting for, and nothing of importance was decided except by the people on Assembly; generals were elected or ostracized, armies and ships sent out, reports from the far-flung front considered and more triremes built. And not only did the political life continue: the artistic and intellectual life continued too. Sophocles found time to brood on the ultimate problems of human life, and Euripides to expose the folly and hollowness of victory and the ugliness of revenge, and express his loathing of war. Socrates too was in Athens walking the avenues in the Agora (except when he was heroically fighting for democracy at Delium, or saving the life of wounded Alcibiades at the battle of Poteidæa), talking and trying to convince those who would listen that the good of the soul was the supreme good, and that all men were essentially alike and equal.

Sparta made an alliance with her arch-enemy, Persia, whose gold always animated the political marionettes of the Greek city-states. A combined fleet of two hundred ships were now sent along the Asia Minor coast to interrupt the transport of food supplies to Athens from her northern allies and the colonies of the Black Sea regions. The Athenians sent one hundred and eighty triremes manned with their last available crews, to keep open the sea routes of their food supplies. Xenophon, who completed Thucydides' unfinished history of this war, left us a wonderful description of this last tragic battle. After days of cunning maneuvering and deployment, the Spartan ships lured the Athenians into a fatal position, near the Hellespont, and virtually destroyed them all.

Beaten by land and sea, Athens was forced to sue for peace. The Spartan allies would give her peace on the terms they now specified, namely, Athens must destroy her walls and limit her fleet to twelve vessels, and must also acknowledge the leadership of Sparta. Without ships, without allies and without provisions, Athens could only yield—"and so they fell to leveling the fortifications and the Long Walls with much enthusiasm, to the accompaniment of female flute players, deeming that day the beginning of liberty to Greece." But it was the beginning of the death of classic Greece.

The long and frequent wars broke the power of one State after another. The Peloponnesian War had ended in the overthrow of the leadership of Athens. The Corinthian War ten years later (395-387 B.C.) broke Corinth. And the short-lived power of Sparta was ended when she was defeated by Thebes in the battle of Leuctra in 379 B.C. Thebes was no more successful.

Constant strife had weakened the country, and when a younger and stronger power which was steadily growing up on her northern border, made its appearance on the scene, in the person of Philip of Macedon, the Greek city-states could offer very little resistance. Happily, though, the Macedonians were people of a kindred stock.

Athens—democracy itself—failed. Pericles the greatest and wisest of all Athenian statesmen, knew it might be so: "I am more afraid" he said, "of our own blunders than of the enemy's devices." And he was right.

Let us now put aside for a time the story of wars and empires, and take up the story of science and philosophy. Philosophy is a Greek word, a compound from philo (I love) and sophia (wisdom). Most of our vocabulary which has to do with education is derived from the Greek. To students of the history of ideas, most roads lead to Athens. Three men who profoundly modified thinking were Socrates, Plato and Aristotle. And if one studies the history of physics, biology, or political philosophy, or aesthetics, one begins with Democritus, Euclid and Archimedes.

For the Greek thinkers, the universe is essentially rational and logical; it has form, can be seen and understood. Whatever is abstract or general is a deduction from observation of fact, whatever is irrational belongs to the realm of illusion. Think of it, it is this basic point of view which not only produced a theory about the world itself, but furnished the basic concept which would permit scientific progress. Greek philosophy begins with an inquiry into the first cause or the essence of the objective world, and is largely interested in external nature, but gradually turns its eye inward, on man himself, and is then called "humanistic." Its first problem is: What is nature, therefore, man? its second: What is man, and therefore, nature? And shifting interest this way from nature to man himself raised innumerable new issues for discussion, ethics, religion, psychology and other questions. This philosophic discussion about nature and man and the universe, started by the Greek people, continued for more than a thousand years, from about 585 B.C. to 529 A.D. when the Christian Byzantine emperor Justinian closed the schools of philosophy.

While men all over the Greek world were searching for truth in this way, and a growing tendency toward freedom and individualism was developing everywhere, Athens was growing to a world-power. It was the last half of the fifth century B.C., the great age of enlightenment.

The great economic changes and the establishing of democratic institutions had given a further impetus to independent thought and action, and with these came the desire for power, wealth, culture and fame, and above all education. Traditional views of religion, morality, science, were subject to criticism. The demand for instruction was stronger than ever before. Public life in Athens offered a splendid field for skilled men, and brought thither a class of people from the colonies of Asia Minor and southern Italy who took up teaching as a profession. They are called Sophists or "wisdom mongers." The term Sophist originally meant a wise and skilful man, but gradually lost its meaning, and became a term of reproach partly because the Sophists took pay, partly owing to the shallow teaching and fantastic views of some of the later Sophists. They taught many subjects, from grammar to astronomy, but oratory was their main subject, because it was considered the best passport to sure success in life. In general their teaching was superficial, and people were shown how to embellish their speeches with elegant phrases, and how to work on the finer feelings of a jury, or how to move an audience, and above all how to meet and argue a given point, regardless of the truth or falsehood in it. In other words, as Aristophanes complains, "how to make the worse appear the best cause." Among all who debated and questioned the wisdom of such teaching by the Sophists, by far the greatest was Socrates, and this is his story:

Socrates was born in Athens, 469 B.C. the son of poor parents. He first took up sculpture, but soon felt "a divine vocation to examine himself by questioning other men." He was short, stocky and stout, blear-eyed and snub-nosed, and had a large mouth and thick lips. The saintly little philosopher was shabbily dressed, careless in his appearance, and uncouth, but these peculiarities were soon forgotten when he began to speak. He was subtle and keen, quick to detect a fallacy in an argument and skilful in steering the course of the conversation to the very heart of the matter. And he was kind and gentle, brimming over with good humor.

Socrates was the great cross-examiner. He charged no fee and as a result fell into the direst poverty. But still he continued his quest for truth and his discussions of the problems concerning man's search for wisdom. And though he wrote nothing, he is the source from which shoot out the divergent streams of thought identified with the various later schools. When he learned that his friend Chærephon had gone to Delphi to ask the oracle whether any man was wiser than Socrates, and was told that no man was wiser, Socrates declared, "I then decided that the oracle meant that those people are wisest who, like me, know that their wisdom amounts to nothing." Again and again he would say, "One thing I know, that I know nothing," even though he was the man who brought order into the intellectual and moral chaos of his age, sifted the true from the false, the essential from the accidental, and set men right and helped them see things in their right relations. "I know nothing," said one of the greatest figures in the history of thought, the intellectual father of a long line of thinkers whose ideas and ideals dominated the world of thought for two thousand years and continue to influence speculation of Western civilization to this day.

Socrates loved Athens, and lived in that city nearly all his life, except when he joined the army, and fought at Delion and in the battle of Potidæa, where he saved the life of Xenophon the historian. In 406 B.C. he was made one of the Senate of Five Hundred, and had other honors accorded him, continuing his teaching alternately with his public duties. He would come to the Agora, or to one of the great Gymnasia, and always a following would gather around him. His normal method was always to proceed by question and answer. He called everything to question, "What is happiness?" or "How is man to find happiness in life?—What is good life?—What is courage, truth, heroism?—What is friendship?—What is this or that?—Justice, piety, the noble and the base, the beautiful and the ugly?" Carefully he guided his listeners to the root of the question, searching with them to find the truth of the matter; he taught them to trust their reason. He discussed a question with his pupils but he never lectured to them or dictated his own convictions and ideas.

For more than thirty years Socrates guided the Athenians to find truth. He had a following of young people who loved his keen logic and clear wisdom and delighted in listening to his wise sayings, his spirited wit and charming dialogue, and were devoted to him. But there were others who thought him harmful to the State, claiming that some of his followers had caused great harm to Athens, take for instance his friend Alcibiades the traitor and Critias the tyrant. More and more fathers grumbled that their sons wasted their time in the Gymnasia listening to Socrates; and more serious were the charges of some people who were startled by Socrates' strange voice and reasoning, his odd ways, and unorthodox words.

In 399 B.C. an Athenian citizen charged Socrates with impiety. He was publicly accused in the Assembly of introducing new gods and new ideas. The penalty was death. He could easily have escaped but chose to remain and stand trial before a jury of 501 Athenian citizens. Socrates spoke to the jury as was customary. He spoke of an inner voice, of his service in war, and in peace to the city he loved so well, for care and interest to questions that pertain not to money-making, but wisdom, and truth and the perfection of soul and mind. He said, he did not run away from his post in time of war, and his duty to mankind in time of peace, indeed it would be strange conduct for a man of truth, if he were to run away, through fear of death for doing what God had commanded him to do, in searching for truth and beauty. He spoke and ended his talk with these words: "I shall not change my way of life, even if I may die for it many times. And to you and to God I entrust my cause to decide it as is best for God, for you, and for me."

But he was found guilty by a majority of sixty votes and then was asked to propose some other form of punishment, in accordance with the law. Socrates refused. He refused to go into exile or to pay a fine. Was it a crime to teach the truth, to seek truth? His many friends and pupils visited him in prison. On the day of his death they came early at dawn. On this day they were to lose a father, a wise man, a counsellor, a true and great friend. Would he escape if they would help him? No! no! that's not the way; nor would he be sad at his death—

the journey of his soul to a new world. He prayed then, and drank the hemlock, one method of death in Athens—and died. This was the end of the wisest and probably the finest man of all ancient Greece.

While Socrates devoted himself to the care, and welfare of men's minds, another great man devoted his life to the care of men's bodies. His name is Hippocrates, and he is called the Father of Medicine. He was nine years younger than Socrates, and born in the tiny island of Cos, which was the center of medical learning. He traveled to many places and came to Athens by invitation to help combat the plague. The school and sanatorium which he founded were still the greatest medical center even under the Ptolemies centuries later. Hippocrates was the first ancient doctor to practise his profession as doctors do today, with a scientific outlook, free from guess-work and quackery and to maintain a high standard of ethics, still observed by physicians the world over who take the Hippocratic Oath.

Socrates' greatest disciple and most devoted follower was Plato. He was the son of noble parents, and was 23 years old when Socrates was executed. Plato spent the rest of his long life teaching and writing Socratic dialogues. He is said to have traveled in Egypt, to have visited Italy and to have lived for a time at the court of Dionysios I, the tyrant of Syracuse, who became his enemy and sold him into slavery as a prisoner of war: all these stories have been denied. But this we know: while his teacher before him spoke mostly in the Agora, Plato selected a school in the groves near Athens, shaded with trees, and provided with fountain water. This was the famous Academy, where he taught mathematics and different branches of philosophy, by means of a method that has been compared to our modern seminar. After Plato's death, the Academy was continued by his pupils, and was a great center of learning for nearly a thousand years.

Emerson has said that Plato "stands on a path that has no end, but runs continually around the universe." He did much thinking and writing of his own ideas, on government and education; man's mind and soul, the nature of truth, goodness, virtue and the divine cause of all things. Socrates, turning from natural philosophy, emphasized the

great importance of man himself, his mind and soul. It was this work
which was continued by Plato. He taught that Socrates' "divine soul"
is the ultimate source of all life. His philosophy is rationalistic, in the
sense that it affirms the existence of a real world; a rational knowledge
of the universe is possible, and of knowledge itself and all things. The
universe is, at bottom, a rational universe: a spiritual system. Plato's
great book, *The Republic,* is an ideal of a perfect state. In the *Timæus*
Plato deals with time, the universe, and the principle of matter, and
the world-soul in an attempt to explain the origin of nature. Plato's
convincing demonstrations of the eternal value and importance of the
ideal are one of the greatest assertions of the human spirit.

In the student body at Plato's Academy there was a brilliant young
pupil who became the most famous exponent of pure logic. This was
Aristotle, son of the court physician of Philip of Macedon. At the age
of seventeen he entered Plato's Academy, where he remained for
twenty years as student an [1] teacher. In 342 he was called by King
Philip to direct the education of his son Alexander. Seven years later
he returned to Athens, and established a school. He was a man of
noble character, realizing in his own personality the Greek ideal of
measure and harmony embodied in his system of ethics. His love for
truth was strong; his judgment sober, acute, impartial. He worked
with calm, impersonal reason. He is one of the greatest figures in the
history of thought. Among his most important works are his treatises
on Logic, Ethics, Rhetoric, Poetics, Politics, Physics, and Metaphysics.
In the latter part of the 19th century his long-lost work *The Constitution of Athens* was discovered.

Chapter Eight

THE ALEXANDRIAN WORLD
(336-31 B.C.)

ON THE northern border of Greece a new power, Macedonia, was growing. The shrewd King Philip made a plea to unite and control the Greek world. There were some people in Athens who were now urging the city-states to unite under Philip and march against Persia; but the famous orator Demosthenes violently attacked the Macedonian as a barbarian, in a series of speeches known as "The Philippics." His advice prevailed and the cities in a long struggle against Macedon were finally defeated at Chæronea (338 B.C.). Philip then presented himself as leader of all Greece and revealed his plan to free the Ionian cities from Persia. Two years later, when he was about to set out, he died, and his young son Alexander succeeded to the throne.

Alexander was one of the most astonishing young men the world has ever known. From childhood he was intrigued by the mysteries of life; daydreamed of cities that lay beyond the horizon, and wanted to know the shape of the earth, what lay to the east, and what to the west. At the boy's most plastic age, his father brought Aristotle from Athens as his tutor. In the grassy walks and terraces of the garden the blond youth sauntered beside his "genius of logic," asking endless questions, explaining how he had learned to love and cherish the *Iliad* and how he revered Achilles. He expounded metaphysics with the solemnity of fourteen. Aristotle gave him a new copy of Homer, annotated by his own hand, which Alexander carried with him on all his campaigns. He is said to have slept with the *Iliad* and his dagger under his pillow.

Aristotle roused in him an interest in nature, science, medicine and literature.

Macedonia was too small for Alexander. At the age of twenty, upon his father's death, he marched south to Corinth, where he was recognized by all the city-states, except Sparta, as commander-in-chief, and won the allegiance of his father's army.

He was clearing the northwest when a report spread through the cities of the south that Alexander had died. Persian gold had persuaded Thebes to rise against the Macedonian garrison, and other states were contemplating revolt. At a speed no army before had attempted, Alexander's troops appeared before the walls of Thebes, captured it, and razed it to the ground, sparing only the temples and Pindar's house. By destroying Thebes, Alexander cowed the Greek cities and ended all resistance. But they were treated leniently.

He then set forth to conquer the whole of the known world, and as the world, in his day, lay to the east, he marched in that direction. Where was he going? To conquer the Persian Empire? Did he know how big and powerful it was? Yes, he had some faint idea about it, but it didn't really matter, for this boy believed himself to be the son of Zeus and an invincible god.

We know how he looked and what he did when he leapt off the pontoon on the farther shore of the Bosphorus. He was sunburnt and blond, not tall nor heavy, and was quick of eye; his head leaned a bit to one side. He rode his favorite horse, Bucephalus, in battle, and fought with the cavalry. His favored weapon was a light sword with a razor edge. His mounting of his horse was always the signal for the charge. The only armor he wore was a quilted coat and an iron helmet polished like silver.

His first act when he landed was to go to Troy and sacrifice to Achilles, his great ancestor. Then on to conquer Persia, whose king was young Darius III, a handsome figure but not to be compared with the great Darius who had invaded Greece a century and a half before. His empire extended from the Upper Nile to the Indus, from Samarkand to Babylon, from the Caspian to the Red Sea. It had absorbed and held the lands of all its predecessors: Assyria, Egypt, Babylon, the country of the Lydians, the Phrygians, the Armenians, the Jews, the Hyrcanians, Parthians, Bactrians, with their wealth, their capitals, and their gods, and in its greatest extent on the north it held Thrace in Europe and the Ionian cities along the Asia Minor coast. Its rulers from the far-flung borders of the empire had the waters of three great rivers, the Nile, the Indus, and the Danube brought and mingled together in a golden bowl in the palace of Susa as a symbol of their possession. Darius was king of kings, his riches fabulous, his army enormous. Against all this might, what did Alexander have? An army of about forty thousand men, well disciplined, and a fantastic belief in himself and his destiny.

Alexander devoted some time to securing the principal Ionian cities, won a spectacular victory at Granicus and came to Gordium, where there was an ancient chariot in the temple, the yoke of which was fastened by an intricate knot of many cords made of the bark of the cornel tree. The oracle had said that whoever would untie this knot would rule the world. Alexander drew his sword and with a stroke slashed it through.

Marching southeast, he came to the Cilician Gates, a narrow pass between mountains, and put to flight the garrison guarding it. Near the entrance to Syria, Darius had assembled a huge army. The two forces faced each other across a river in the plain of Issus. Though out-numbered twenty to one, Alexander maneuvered the Imperial army into a space much too narrow for its great numbers, rendering them ineffective. He then attacked at night, far off the main wing to avoid being enveloped by sheer numbers of this human tide. By dawn the Imperial army was torn to pieces and the roads for leagues around blocked by scattered battalions and mobs of fugitives. When the news spread that Darius had fled, the whole Persian army retreated.

Darius left behind an immense quantity of booty, which Alexander distributed to his troops; but Darius' tent, chariot and crown were reserved for him. "Here," says Plutarch, "when Alexander came to the high pavilion of embroidered silk and beheld the basins, vials, boxes and vases curiously wrought in gold, the crystal bath, the enameled censers that still smoked, for everything had been left in order and untouched, the tables at which the satraps dined, he turned to those present and said, 'Now this then, it seems, it is to be a king.' When he heard wailing from an adjoining pavilion, and was told it came from the king's mother and family, Alexander sent this message: 'Darius is still alive, and you yourselves, and the people of Persia have nothing to fear.' "

Alexander did not follow Darius, but marched south through Syria to Tyre, where a strong Phœnician fleet refused to submit. Tyre was a naval base on an island offshore, protected by high walls of stone two miles in circumference. Its capture would permit Alexander's army to continue safely to Egypt and Mesopotamia. He was obliged to lay siege to it for seven months, but left it in ruins.

When he had conquered Syria and Palestine, Alexander entered Egypt. He respected the gods of all peoples and sacrificed to local deities, as he came across their shrines. Egypt, which was part of the Persian Empire, welcomed and proclaimed him Pharaoh. Egypt he loved; and henceforth divided his interest between the West and the East. He was so pleased by the ideal location of a fishing village on the delta of the Nile to which he had come in his sight-seeing trips around Egypt that without delay he ordered streets to be laid out and a city built on the Macedonian plan. He gave this city his own name. Alexander did not merely conquer for booty and plunder. His army was followed by another army of traders, scientists, and scholars. At strategic points he stopped long enough to found a town, a city or a trading post.

After a year's rest, he gave the signal which set the Macedonian machine rolling northeast across the Euphrates to the Tigris. The Persian king had collected a second army, which engaged Alexander's forces in the dreadful battle of Arbela and was completely cut to pieces. In 331 B.C. Alexander entered in triumph Darius' three magnificent capitals: Babylon, Susa and Persepolis.

Alexander loved Greek culture and the Greek spirit, and wanted to spread it over the world. And he knew how to make friends. He obeyed the laws and observed the religion of each country. He turned over the rule of conquered peoples to native leaders. He would join together Greeks, Persians, Egyptians—any people—to build one world-state. But when he filled gaps in his army with foreigners, some of his own men complained; and some were suspected of rebellion. Still, he advanced eastward against the advice and wishes of his officers and men. Not understanding his purpose, they thought him mad.

In 328 B.C., Alexander crossed the snow-capped Hindu Kush Mountains into the upper valley of the Indus. In less than a year he had brought his army practically intact through the Khyber Pass and a labyrinth of mountains inhabited by fierce ancestors of Pathans and Afghans. As soon as he arrived at the Indus he met in battle with Maharajah Porus, who according to Plutarch was nearly seven feet high, and rode on a huge elephant. He was a brave man, and with great difficulty did Alexander overcome him in a hard-fought battle. Near the scene of this battle Bucephalus, Alexander's horse died, and in his memory a city called Bucephala was founded. Alexander was now at Beas (northern India). He had gone more than 2,000 miles beyond the Greek maps of his time.

On a hilltop in the extreme north of Samarkand he peered across the horizon, and was undecided. There were records of a river Ganges somewhere beyond. He wanted to find it and record his findings for geographers. Did its waters flow into the Oceanos of mythology, which encircled the world? What about the people, the land, animals, plants, mines? Were there any great cities there?

At this point his men refused to follow him. They had been marching and fighting for nearly eight years. They were tired from many battles, thirsty marches through mountains and desolate plains, weary of the endless drudgery, and monotony, the founding of towns along the line, the dull wounds, the homesickness. Alexander had grown restless and irritated. He peered across the Indus River into the darkness—and turned back. The army returned through lower Baluchistan, but he and a few troops took a longer way round, to explore the mouth of the Indus. At Babylon, Alexander contracted a fever and died. It was the summer of 323 B.C. and he was thirty-three years old.

The world was never the same after this extraordinary man. He had sowed the seeds of Greek culture through all of Western Asia, where they grew to modify the ideas and customs of future civilizations. His successors were unable to maintain control of the vast area he had conquered and though waves of Roman, Arabian, Tartar and Ottoman conquests swept over these lands—none of the conquerors were able wholly to eradicate the influence of Greek culture, or to exterminate that element of population which was of Greek blood and ancestry. To this day traces of Greek influence are found everywhere in that wide part of the earth.

The period between the conquests of Alexander and the absorption of the Greek world by the Roman Empire shortly before the opening of the Christian Era is called the Hellenistic Age, because of the influence Greek culture had on other civilizations. The new cosmopolitan centers of society were the foundations of Macedonian kings in lands beyond the Aegean: Alexandria, Antioch, Pergamus, Ephesus and Rhodes.

By far the most outstanding was Alexandria, a remarkable city whose culture was part Greek, part Egyptian, part Oriental, famed for its scholars, its library, its luxury—but never a part of Greece proper.

Chapter Nine

THREE EMPIRES

(31 *B.C.*-1821 *A.D.*)

I

ROME, unlike Greece, had all the qualities for empire building and organization. From the earliest days of the Republic, Rome showed her genius in making not only great roads but great laws to meet the growing needs of her state. The whole Empire was soon brought together under one Roman law, which later became the basis of the legal systems of most states of Europe.

On the other hand, the Greeks did achieve a unity of civilization—which was far more binding than political unity. It has held them together to this day. In every domain of thought the Greeks were masters and models, the first teachers who designed the cultural pattern of Europe. Horace, the Roman poet, said: "Greece, conquered, took her uncivilized conqueror captive."

During the first period of Roman rule, Greece was despoiled and exploited. When the Empire was established, Greece was made an integral part of it and shared Rome's greatness. Cæsar refounded Corinth almost exactly one hundred years after Mummius had destroyed it and had strewn salt for miles around the ruins. Augustus and his successors rebuilt the temples. Athens became again an important place. Pilgrims and tourists, officials and scholars went there in numbers.

In the reign of Augustus, Jesus had been born in Judæa, and when Augustus died no one in Rome could yet know that Jesus was to bring a new age into the whole world. The number of His followers continued to grow. To the masses the good news of a God who cared for all seemed like a glimpse of heaven. Many Jewish and Greek people were converted. One of these was Paul, born at Tarsus, in Asia Minor, about the same time that Jesus was born at Bethlehem. Tarsus was a center of culture. And being of a well-to-do family, Paul received the finest education. He spoke Greek and wrote it fluently.

By the end of the first century, Jesus was given an additional name, "Christos." The teachings of Jesus Christ were soon thoroughly Hellenized and his followers were called Christians. Among the very first converts were some Greek intellectuals; the number of these increased as time went on. Greek philosophy was made the background of Christian doctrine and the Greek language became its vehicle for universal expression. Of the four Gospels, three were originally composed in Greek, and the fourth, probably written in Aramaic, soon appeared in a Greek version.

By the third century, Christians were to be found in all parts of the Empire, in some places nearly half the population, and were well organized, with bishops who met in council periodically. We call them Fathers of the Church. The Romans were essentially a tolerant people, but conflict sometimes arose when the Christians clashed with followers of other religions. The early Christians were militant; they had to be. Quite often the Roman authorities had to step in and restore order. The repetition of such disturbances caused persecutions of the Christians, on a small scale in various parts of the Empire. In 249, under Emperor Decius, they suffered the first general persecution, which was followed by another in a few years. But it did not matter; the arenas did not terrify them. Men and women of all classes by tens of thousands met their death, but the faithful grew in number and grew stronger. Persecutions made more martyrs for the faith and proved the very seed of the church; Christianity was never in danger of extermination. The last and greatest persecution was begun under Diocletian in A.D. 303. He was determined to put an end by crushing the Christians at all costs.

From the middle of Diocletian's reign, the cæsar who ruled over

Britain and Gaul was Constantius, who made his provinces safe and prosperous, and who refused to persecute the Christians. His son, Constantine, spent his early youth at the other end of the Empire, in the court of Nicomedia, where he learned how the Empire was governed and saw the dangers threatening it from without, and the terror of persecutions tearing it from within. He was an intelligent young man, brave and ambitious. In 305, after Diocletian abdicated, he quickly left the court and made his way across Europe by horse. He met his father, who was now an Augustus, at Boulogne, and both crossed to Eburacum (York) the headquarters of the army in Britain. A year later his father died, and the Roman army in Britain saluted him as Augustus in his father's place. But there were other rivals, and to win the throne he was obliged to fight the armies of rival generals. By 312, he had defeated all of them and become Emperor. Constantine, somehow, did not like Rome. In 330 he moved his capital to the other end of the Empire, to the northeast corner of Greece between the Black Sea and the Sea of Marmora. This was an ideal location; the point of contact from all points of Europe and Asia. There was an ancient Greek town here called Byzantion. Constantine changed its name to Constantinople, and built there magnificent structures. Constantine was fond of pomp and splendor, but he had great ideas of unity, peace, and strong government. He had the courage to make Christianity the state religion and to bring its strength into the tottering empire. He built great churches and held councils to discuss problems confronting the Church, and this greatly helped to keep Christianity alive and strong, and the people united in the midst of the many dangers which were about to engulf the Empire.

One of the most confusing periods in history is that of the great invasions of Europe, during the fourth and fifth centuries. The Teutonic invasion into western and central Europe was nearly at its end when suddenly for some unknown reason wave upon wave of Asiatic peoples poured into Europe through the Caspian Gap. This Asiatic group of tribes, collectively known as the Huns, was made up of kindred peoples, who originally inhabited vast areas in central Asia, Persia and India.

Of all the invaders, the most destructive and dreaded were the hordes of Attila. Collecting his troops on the edge of the Black Forest in Germany, he crossed the Rhine (451) on a bridge of boats, and after terrific destruction and ravage stood on the road to Rome which lay before him open and almost undefended. But he allowed himself to be bought off by an embassy of Roman citizens.

By the middle of the fifth century, Roman power had shrunk so much that anyone could easily cross the border; Roman authority, now limited to central Gaul and Italy, was fast disappearing altogether. In the next fifty years even these areas were lost to various Germanic tribes. This was no sudden invasion but rather the last act of a long drama. Thousands of Germans entered the Empire as household servants; others were brought home as slaves by the Roman legions, and still others were made Roman soldiers. After the sack of Rome by the Vandals, the Roman troops in Italy were mainly Germans, who now did their own making of rulers, by setting up a succession of puppet emperors. The long line of Cæsars ended in 476 when the puppet emperor, the child Romulus, "abdicated." In 493, Theodoric, leader of the Goths, founded the first East Gothic kingdom and ruled the Western Roman Empire.

II

In the East, another empire, which centered round the city of Constantinople, lived on for a thousand years after the one in the West ended. Some historians call this the Eastern Roman Empire, but it wasn't Roman at all. It was Roman politically—Rome ruled, that is, for a few centuries, but even then it was Greek in language and religion, and Greek-Oriental in spirit. Constantinople had displaced Rome itself. Its culture was now Christian; Greek civilization had assimilated Christianity. One of the most surprising events of world history is the gradual transformation of the Eastern Roman Empire into the Greek Byzantine Empire, testifying to the vigor of the Greek mind and the vitality of Greek civilization. The Byzantine Empire stood as the bulwark between Europe and successive attacks of barbarian hordes issuing again and again out of the "dead heart of Asia." In the darkest centuries of Europe, the Byzantines cast a light to remote corners of the world.

Byzantine civilization was primarily an urban civilization. The East was always famous for its opulent cities, their size, their luxury and their strength. Constantinople was all of these and the inheritor and preserver of an intellectual tradition as well. Great because of its strategic position, it became the center of three worlds: Greek, Asian and Roman. The population grew rapidly to nearly a million inhabitants. The great open-air markets were thronged with merchants of every nationality. Surrounded by water east, north, and south, the city is exposed to attack by land only on the west. This side was protected by stupendous walls and towers, some four miles long. Besides these walls near the city, an outer wall had been built as a first line of defense. In places the barricades were two hundred feet thick and one hundred feet high, with several parts rising tier above tier to permit concerted action, and always alive with large bodies of troops ready to pour down arrows, huge stones or liquid fire. Constantinople was practically impregnable and for more than a thousand years, besieged many a time by barbarian hordes, was never taken by direct assault, not even by the vast Saracen army led by Moslemah in 717. Constantinople thrust them all back, and delayed for centuries the advance of Islam into Europe. It gave time to the small and weak European states yet in their formative period to develop culturally and politically in the present line. The repulse of the Arabs was a turning point in the history of Europe.

It was not until the spring of the year 1453 when Mohammed II, Sultan of the Ottomans, appeared before Constantinople at the head of 250,000 men supported by an immense blockading fleet. Cut off altogether from the outside world, the defending garrison of about seven thousand men met the foe. Though small and weak it was heroic, and the walls high and strong. The fleet of thirteen warships was well manned, and the initial assaults and bombardments were repulsed one after another. The Sultan then decided on a grand attack by land and by sea, and his heralds proclaimed May 28th as the day. Trumpets pealed on the eve of the grand assault, and fires lit the sky all about the beleaguered city. The dawn was filled with cries of anguish as death met the hordes rushing to storm the barricades. Two hours of fierce fighting followed. The walls were high and strong. The defenders were brave. Then suddenly one of the most famous incidents in all history took place: the *Kerkoporta* (gate of fluted wood), long since blocked up to frustrate a prophecy that the conqueror of the city would enter by it, had been opened up to facilitate a sortie, and was somehow left open and undefended. A roaming band of Turks found it and poured into the city. The defenders rushed to the gate and tried to close it while cries arose: "The Turks! The Turks are in the city!" Panic followed.

Meanwhile Mohammed, noticing the confusion and disorder at the gate, commenced flogging his men till the walls were scaled and the hordes poured in. Alone among his fallen warriors Emperor Constantine Palaelogos XI looked about him and cried: "Is there no Christian to take my head?" No one heard him, for not one Christian stood near him alive. He was struck by an Arab blade, to fall among his warriors.

After the fall of Constantinople, most of the Greek people with some means fled to western Europe. For decades after, during the dark days of depression that followed, Greek refugees roamed Europe seeking a haven. Among them were scholars and teachers, artists and craftsmen, who came with their manuscripts and their treasury of art and learning. They settled mostly in Florence, Venice and other Italian cities.

The fifteenth century is a century of new enlightenment. To this the Greek people made their contribution. The educated men of Constantinople were steeped in classic knowledge, which they brought with them when they fled after their capital's fall.

III

But all the Greek people did not flee. The mass of common people remained on the lands of their fathers, disarmed and reduced to serfdom. In 1456, Athens was captured by the Turks. The Parthenon became a Turkish mosque. By the end of the century all of Greece, except for a few Venetian provinces in the Peloponnesus was under Turkish rule, and was divided into districts called *pashalics*, each under the jurisdiction of a Pasha or a Bey, all powerful and responsible for his acts only to the Sultan.

The Ottoman rulers allowed no means for the development of the enslaved people's minds. Slowly darkness set in. The mass of the common people of the Balkan peninsula lived through four hundred years of suppression. No wonder that Lord Byron after his first visit to Greece, said: " 'Tis Greece but living Greece no more." There was one class of these poor people who fled to the many Greek mountains. They were the famous patriot-warriors known to history as the Kleftes, who lived in open rebellion with the Turkish authorities. They held councils in remote mountain areas, lived in caves coming out and acting under cover of darkness. They braved the Turkish armies, often raided their camps, and engaged them in battles on mountain passes where superior numbers did not count. They became the terror of the Turkish authorities and were declared outlaws. They became the vanguard in the struggle for freedom. Every Greek mountain, its peak or its cave was the abode of a band of Kleftsmen.

As the years of slavery rolled on, the pillars of wisdom were felled one by one; ideals uprooted. The entire race was dragged into the mire. The only ray of hope was the Church; the only means of preserving the language and customs. It became the medium which transmitted age-old traditions from generation to generation. The Church was the center of life in the community. Where schools were not allowed openly, they existed in secret. If books were not available the church still had Bibles and Psalteries. From these the people were taught to know the truth; to know their language.

History records, during the four centuries of Turkish rule, sixteen sporadic uprisings and three major revolts. Never did the Greek people stop fighting for freedom. In 1770 took place the bloodiest revolt. This was during the Russo-Turkish war waged by Catherine the Great (1768-1774). Urged on and encouraged by the appearance of the Russian fleet in the Mediterranean, Greek patriots set up an independent state in southern Greece. But when the war ended, they were left to the mercy of their masters. Wholesale massacres followed.

As the years rolled on, the vitality of the Ottoman Empire began to wane. By the latter part of the 17th century, a gradual breakdown of its administration set in. The Empire was often called "the sick man of Europe." The question now was, who would succeed it, and who would take its vast territories.

Chapter Ten

A NEW NATION
(1821-1952)

THE LAST part of the 18th century was an era of struggle for freedom and equality. The American Revolution and the French Revolution inspired hope and confidence among all oppressed peoples. In Greece there was a strong undercurrent of rebellion. Rigas Pheraios appeared on the scene, singing his fiery songs, calling on all the Balkan peoples to rise against the Ottoman Empire. Captured in Trieste, Rigas was turned over to the Turkish authorities in 1796, and two years later was executed, the first martyr to Greek freedom.

After that, for twenty-five years, strengthened by events abroad and their position of economic dominance in the Ottoman Empire, the Greeks became increasingly bent on gaining their freedom.

A day celebrated by Greeks every year is March 25th, the anniversary of their first step toward independence. On that day in 1821 the Metropolitan of Patras blessed the banner of revolution at the monastery of Agia Lavra and called on all to join in the struggle. Patriots in Greece and all over Europe had banded together in a secret organization established at Odessa in 1814. Wherever Greek people lived, thousands were initiated into its secret activities.

Liberty or Death was the battle cry of peasants, fishermen and all men who were weary of foreign masters. Intimately acquainted with their rugged mountains of death-trap crags and passes, they began a guerrilla war, using age-old tactics to harass and exasperate and wear down the enemy. A few men in the Aegean, on three tiny islands, were able to dominate the eastern Mediterranean. In the mountains of

Macedonia, Epirus, Thessaly and Peloponnesus the campaign was carried on by bold raids of infantry.

At first the Great Powers in Europe frowned on the Greek revolt and believed it would quickly be crushed. Instead they were almost immediately astonished by the success of the insurgents, then, alarmed and impelled to come to the aid of Turkey. Since the fall of Napoleon, the Holy Alliance, dominated by Prince Metternich, Chancellor of Austria—one of the four great powers at that time—had discussed the claims and aspirations of each power at various conferences, without ever taking thought of the rights of the Balkan people. The Powers were concerned about the "status quo," that is, the peace of Europe; and each member of the Holy Alliance pledged to maintain it. Already two uprisings had been crushed, one in southern Italy and one in Spain. Then came the Greek war. It could not achieve any good, Metternich contended; the real cause of his antagonism lying in Austria's desire to expand eastward, on areas of the Ottoman Empire. But here Russia had direct interest, too.

The Czars believed themselves to be the natural protectors of the Patriarchate of Constantinople, and of the Christian populations in the Ottoman Empire. They had received Christianity from Constantinople, and their cultural traditions were still Byzantine. And the peoples of the Balkans were mostly of the same Orthodox Church. The Greek War for Independence caused great embarrassment to Metternich, because it thrust a wedge between Austrian interests and Russian. He, therefore, scoffed at the Greek people, then denounced them for disturbing the peace, and finally kept Czar Alexander from coming to their aid as he had planned. Under Metternich's pressure, the Great Powers, at the conference of Leybach characterized the Greek Revolution as "criminal" and the Greek patriots fighting a life to death struggle for freedom as "brigands." Some governments went even as far as to decree death penalty for those caught in mere communication with the "rebels!"

The only country which ardently and from the outset of war shared the faith of the Greek people and opened its heart to the Greek cause was the United States of America. And from the beginning, too, Lord Byron, the great English poet, exhorted the world to go to the aid of Greece, through his poems and through correspondence with the great men of his time. America first, and then other nations responded. The first head of a nation to speak out in favor of the Greek people was President James Monroe. In his message to Congress on December 4, 1822, in a plea for the Greek cause, Monroe gave expression to America's sentiment, and at the same time expressed the hope that the Mother of Democracy would regain her equal place among the civilized nations: "The name of Greece fills the mind and heart with the highest and noblest sentiments. The disappearance of this country for a long time under an aggressive dark yoke has profoundly grieved the generous spirits of the past; it was therefore natural for the reappearance of this people in its original character, fighting for its liberty, to arouse sympathy everywhere in the United States."

The halls of Congress rang with vigorous and friendly messages from noted Americans. Edward Everett and John Quincy Adams aroused worldwide interest in the Greek cause. Early in December of 1823, Daniel Webster introduced a resolution to defray the expenses of an agent to Greece, and five weeks later delivered his celebrated oration on Greek independence. It was tantamount to recognition of Greece as an independent state, before that independence was won. Henry Clay applauded Monroe's stand, supported Webster's resolution, and himself made spirited attacks on the Holy Alliance.

The bravery of the Greek warriors struggling against heavy odds; the suffering of the people; and the ruthlessness of the Turkish authorities in their efforts to discourage the insurgents, brought about a wonderful upsurge of enthusiasm for Greek people all over Europe, and strengthened the sentiment of America. Interest heightened even more when reports reached America that the Greek people had established a Federal Constitution, and had elected senators and representatives. Committees had been organized in many cities throughout the United States. Money, provisions, medical supplies were on the way to Greece. Cargo after cargo was shipped out until the war ended.

In Europe, too, a stream of volunteers flowed in swelling volume toward the Aegean.

Lord Byron arrived at Missolonghi in January 1824 to participate actively in the war. Five months before, Markos Botsaris and three hundred Souliotes, after a march of forty miles, had sprung a night attack and routed the vanguard of four thousand Turkish troops advancing to reinforce Missolonghi's besiegers. The town was saved, though Botsaris was killed. Shortly after, Athens was captured and the Acropolis freed from the Turkish garrison. Europe and America were electrified. But Byron now found Greece in greater danger from within, than from the enemy or from without. The old Greek individualism and inability to co-operate was apparent. The leaders were not united among themselves. They were undecided as to leadership and strategy. Byron plunged into the confused counter efforts and intrigues and began to establish a unified command.

He organized a body of 500 Souliotes under his leadership and set up a network of spies in Turkish occupied areas. Guards and sentries were bought off at strategic points, information on the military moves of the enemy was received almost as soon as their decisions were made. Julius Millingen, a young Austrian doctor attached to the army of western Greece, described Missolonghi as a town of about 800 houses, scattered close to the seaside, on a marshy and unhealthy site scarcely above the level of the water. Marshes and pools were mosquito infested, and fever was destined to take Byron's life. The month of January is the heart of the rainy season in Greece. Everything seemed to turn to mud. But Byron would not swerve from his purpose. He identified himself completely with the struggle of Greece, and his words were to be prophetic: "If Greece should fall, I will bury myself in its ruins. If she should establish her independence, I will take up my residence in some part or other—perhaps in Attica." But in April, Byron died, and sealed his passion for Greece. Perhaps his death and America's support were the two salient factors which brought about victory.

Greece's greatest champion in America was Dr. Samuel Gridley

Howe, who arrived in Greece in 1825. He caught the flame of Byron's attachment to Greece. He was appointed surgeon-in-chief of the Greek forces. His services were invaluable.

The early 19th century in America is known as the "Greek Revival" period; and coincided with the Greek Revolution. The American Declaration of Independence, and the adoption of democratic forms of government by the States stimulated interest in classic times. Artists, poets and thinkers, all turned back to the first democracy—to Athens, which in one way or another supplied much of the spirit and cultural background for the newly founded democracy.

In Greece the years 1823-1827 were full of uncertainty, quarrels, reprisals, reverses, followed by sudden victories. Most tragic was the party strife among leaders. Many friends abroad were coming to Greece's help. One was George Canning, the foreign minister of England. He foresaw in the Greek people the power that should eventually replace the declining Ottoman Empire in the southern Balkans. At his sanction the Greeks were able to contract two loans in British markets. Canning was watching for the opportunity to intervene in favor of the Greeks.

The final crisis came when the Sultan of Turkey called on his vessels in Egypt to send their naval and military forces to aid his own. Ibrahim Pasha appeared in the Aegean with a strong force and joined in the third siege of Missolonghi, which lasted for a whole year. Under the compulsion of famine, the garrison made a desperate effort to cut their way through the enemy. On April 22, 1826, three thousand soldiers and over six thousand civilians including women and children, threw themselves on the Turkish lines. Most of them were cut down in the attempt or driven back into the town. The Greeks set fire to powder magazines and blew up friends and foes alike. The cause seemed to be lost. Western Greece was again in the hands of the Sublime Porte. Hopelessness, misery and famine increased with every new foray of the invader. Athens was retaken and the Turko-Egyptian hordes landed in Peloponnesus and embarked upon a new method of stamping out the insurrection by systematically exterminating with sword and fire the whole of the remaining population. The Greeks had expended their utmost efforts, their forces had dwindled, the remnants were exhausted; the hope of freedom was gradually flickering out.

But the British and the French were now pro-Greek. Statesmen were applauding Greek heroism, urging support. It was Canning's moment to step in. He brought about negotiations in Petrograd which resulted in the signing of the first protocol by England and Russia wherein the partial independence of a small part of Greece was recognized. France acceded. A second protocol signed by the three powers called for an armistice between the belligerents and made the Commander of the British fleet the executor. He instantly demanded cessation of hostilities until the Great Powers could confer with Turkey. The Greeks accepted but the Sultan refused, and Ibrahim Pasha did not suspend hostilities. The British Admiral in conjunction with the commanders of the French and Russian fleets in the Aegean then demanded that Ibrahim Pasha leave the port of Pylos and sail to Constantinople. But the Pasha chose to attack the Allied fleet, with the result that on October 20, 1827, the whole of the Turko-Egyptian armada of 120 vessels was destroyed by the combined fleets of England, France and Russia. Turkey ceased to be an important naval power.

Despite this disaster, the Sublime Porte refused to accept the decisions of the Great Powers and called for a general mobilization. The Russo-Turkish War, which had been smoldering for many years, broke out in April. Turkey was completely defeated by Russia, and was forced to accept the Treaty of Adrianople (1829) which secured autonomy for Greece, Serbia, and present-day Rumania. By 1833 the frontiers of Greece had been fixed, the complete independence of the little nation established, and Otto of Bavaria placed on the throne, as a constitutional sovereign.

The Greek War of Independence was one of the important events of the 19th century, producing moral effects throughout the world. It stood for the eviction of the Turks and the restoration of the Byzantine Empire with its old boundaries which included the greater part of the Balkans and all of Asia Minor (Ionia), with Constantinople. Now began a great dramatic conflict. The people's goodwill was strong but the contrast of the greatness of its goal and the poverty of means to achieve it was huge. So the end of the War of Independence was the beginning of a bigger struggle, which was continued through the 19th century and into the 20th. For nearly a century down to the destruction of Smyrna in 1922 the national policy of Greece had as its aim the redemption of the rest of the Greek people under alien rule.

The war came to a successful conclusion in 1830. But the victory affected less than one third of the Greek people in the Turkish Empire. It did not bring freedom to the Greeks of Macedonia, Thrace, Epirus, Crete and the isles of Greece that so thrilled Lord Byron. Even Thessaly, the heart of the little nation, was not included in the map of new Greece, although it had been the scene of the most heroic battles.

The new nation was small, weak and poor. Centuries of misrule had ruined the land. A good many of its resources were left to the Turks. There were nearly eight million Greek people in the Ottoman Empire, whereas free Greece in 1830 included only 750,000 of them, living in a corner of the Greek homeland, which was four-fifths rocks and mountains. But the people who had just won their freedom worked and planned to carry freedom to the millions of the unredeemed Greeks under Ottoman rule. This was accomplished successively, first in 1864 by England's cession of the Ionian Islands in her possession since 1815, and Thessaly by Turkey in 1881, and the acquisition of Macedonia and western Thrace as a result of the Balkan Wars of 1912-1913.

In 1897 there was a Greco-Turkish war which ended in Greece's defeat; it was a heavy blow and it changed the course of the little nation's life. For now a storm of events rapidly succeeded one another. The first phase of this epoch was the Macedonian struggle, which fills the first decade. Bulgarian threat of expansion toward the Aegean with claims upon Macedonia, a threat which has been continued to this day, gave new intensity to Greek national life. A secret war was carried on against the Bulgarians under the very collapsing roof of the Ottoman Empire. It never ended and was never abandoned. The aim was to stabilize the nation and to build up a strong opposition to the Slav block.

The fighting spirit of the "Macedonic plan" as it was called, coincided with the liberal movement in Greek society; a movement found in all activities—political, economic, social and intellectual. In Turkey and Russia, in Egypt, in the Balkans and the Danube basin, the Greek people were flourishing, working, accumulating economic strength, dreaming and cultivating the "Grand Idea" for the liberation of the unredeemed Greek people. A strong section of the capital-owning class with its old ideas of feudal economy was swept away by the new bourgeoisie, made up from the steadily growing middle class. The struggle for a people's government was one with the struggle of the intellectuals for a people's language and literature. It culminated in the civil revolution of 1909, which started a new epoch and brought to the fore a great protagonist.

This new leader was Eleutherios Venizelos (1864-1936), often called "the modern Pericles" for his power of intellect, force of character, eloquence, and dazzling personality.

Venizelos dominated the scene from 1909 to the time of his death. Born in Crete at the time she was fighting her own war of independence, he felt the vicissitudes of the oppressed. The young advocate was transformed into an apostle of nationalism destined to play a most important part in redeeming the Greek people still in bondage. His efforts to liberate the island of his birth revealed his powerful personality. The mainland then turned to him for leadership. Venizelos was invited to take over the reins of the Government with the request that he give the people a new constitution. They found in him a real leader when he took up the challenge and convinced them that there was no need for a new constitution, but a revision of the existing one.

In a few years Venizelos united and modernized Greece; created a good army; extended taxation to all classes progressively; and introduced many reforms. He fathered the Balkan Pact, defeated Bulgaria, and doubled the boundaries of Greece.

The Cretan patriot took the little nation into World War I, upon the right side before it was too late, and thus was able to present her claim and take a seat in the councils of the peace conference of the Treaty of Versailles in 1919. It soon was said in Paris that every time

Venizelos called on Wilson the map of Europe was changed. At the very height of his success, while on his way to Greece with a new map of the Nation, secured at the peace conference of Versailles, he was repudiated by the people he had so faithfully served. It was at a moment when the "Grand Idea" for which the Greek people had been working and planning seemed at last to be realized. Greek frontiers had now jumped the Aegean and taken in half of Asia Minor. But such efforts were too great for the nation's strength. At home a strong reaction was undermining Venizelos' work abroad. It finally succeeded in overthrowing his government at its very peak of accomplishment. At the critical moment when Greece had the greatest need of the genius of the "grand old man" that wise statesman was defeated in the general election in the fall of 1920. Steadily now the national impulse began to weaken and the struggle ended with Greece's defeat in her campaigns in Asia Minor in 1922. This date is the third great milestone in modern Greek history. For the first time since Homeric days the Greek people were compelled to leave Asia Minor and seek refuge in continental Greece. Now the descendants of the earlier Greeks poured into Old Greece from across the Aegean in hundreds of thousands.

The compulsory migration of two million Christians and Moslems, across the Aegean Sea, which followed, was one of history's greatest and most spectacular treks. Of the fleeing multitude nearly one and a half million were Greeks from Anatolia. The absorption of this refugee population is a feat unique in history. An analogy would be an overnight arrival to the shores of the Atlantic seaboard of thirty million people destitute and penniless, who must be housed, fed and clothed, and as soon as possible placed in productive occupations. But here too, Greece's friends came to her rescue. America had a large part in the success of the settlement of these Greek refugees, mostly in Macedonia. In 1923 the League of Nations created the Refugee Settlement Commission, to handle the whole problem. Of its four members, two were Greeks, one British and one American—Henry Morgenthau.

As a result of the Exchange of Minorities, Greece soon was a nation of nearly eight million people, a new fusion and a new population. And

Greece's national policy of redeeming her people under foreign rule was in a way fulfilled. Greece thereafter desired peace, practical peace, and labored for peace with all neighbors. Forgetting the past, she now turned to the east and made friends with her age-old enemy Turkey. The many wars had changed both countries for the better. They both were mellower and more human, ready for understanding. Greece gave a free port in Salonika to Yugoslavia, offered a similar port farther east to Bulgaria and originated the Balkan Entente. Greece even closed her eyes to the ruthless Fascist campaigns, and overlooked Mussolini's plots against her, still hoping and working for peace with all her neighbors.

World War II broke out. On October 28, 1940, Greece's dream for peace was shattered. On that night Count Grazzi, Mussolini's minister in Athens, gave a sumptuous dinner party to distinguished Greek guests. Among them was Metaxas, Prime Minister. It was a cordial, happy gathering; the flags of the two friendly nations were intertwined on the walls and toasts were drunk and pledges made of continued friendship. The party ended late, but not the events of the day. Before dawn Count Grazzi drove to the Prime Minister's home and presented his recent guest with a monstrous ultimatum, demanding entry into the country, and the occupation of strategic sites throughout Greece, including the islands. To all these demands the Greek Minister gave a simple but firm *"Oche!"* which in Greek means "No!" Count Grazzi was quite puzzled by this "No!" "Then this means war," he mumbled. "It does," the Greek Minister assured him laconically. And before the sun rose over the peaks of the Pindus Mountains, the first Fascist legions crossed the frontier from Albania. They were met by the Greek Evzones, fleet mountain troops. Not only were they stopped there but were soon hurled back and pinned against the rocks, ready to be pushed into the Adriatic.

In April, 1941, Greece met a second assault; the Nazi army. Allied troops, British, Australian and New Zealand rushed to help her defend her mountain passes. The new enemy, perhaps, might have been halted had another calamity not then befallen. The Greek people had resisted successively on the Albanian and then on the Bulgarian frontier. But the breakdown of the army of Yugoslavia, which found itself unprepared in the face of infinitely superior forces and material, opened the Greek frontier on the Yugoslav side. This time the Greek army and the Allies had to yield to the Nazi Blitz machine, which had already overrun most of Europe. The Germans streamed through Thermopylæ and reached Athens.

When the Germans took Athens they closed another chapter in the story of Greece. But in those glorious months between October and April little Greece again electrified the civilized world, and once again fulfilled her historic destiny as the citadel of democracy. For it was those months of unexpected resistance that altered the entire Nazi time-table of attack, that saved Moscow by delaying the German assault on Russia till it was too late and "General Winter" took part in the campaign on the side of the Soviets, and gave the British time to reorganize their forces in the eastern Mediterranean and in North Africa.

The victories of the Pindus Mountains and the defense of Thermopylæ were the forerunner of the great Allied coalition which ultimately defeated the Axis. Greece paid for her heroism and her "No!" to the Axis. As soon as the Swastika was flying on the Acropolis, retaliation began. The Germans came as conquerors; the Italians followed; they were joined by the Bulgarians. Famine and death rode on their heels. They picked the country clean as a bone, and announced that the Third German Reich had no responsibility for the feeding of such conquered nations as Greece.

Thereafter, for more than three direful years Greece was completely occupied and made to pay for her love of freedom. Greek history was now an incredible story of endurance. In the face of calculated starvation and disease, the people still found strength to fight. No German was safe; no German slept in peace while in Greece. In 1943 the crisis was reached, with 20 percent of the population dying of starvation. The German army was responsible for the death of some 500,000 Greek people. But in spite of everything, the spirit of resistance stood high. Those who did not join the Greek forces in Egypt and Africa to fight with the British and Australians fled to the mountains and from unscalable hiding places harassed the enemy, in a systematic war of nerves and sabotage.

After four years of starvation and ruthless occupation, Greece was liberated from the Axis in October 1944, still saying *"Oche!"*, still crying: "No!"

Many are the "No's" in Greek history, beginning with the Persian invasions in 490 B.C. They are great symbols of freedom, they help us to find the answer to the question why Greece after thousands of years is still a nation. And the last "No!" we must not lose sight of, for no sooner was one invader a dark dot on the horizon than a new one appeared on Greece's northern borders, more fierce and menacing than the one just gone. He slipped into the nation's political life and was soon demanding leadership by force. He was Marxism. He came insidiously and in the extreme form of Communism, supported and directed by Moscow. He walked the Greek cities and villages, and roamed the land from end to end in the form of terrorism, hatred, wanton slaughter, and moral corruption, but the Greek people are again crying "No!"

Greece is today at an historic crossroads. Blessed with a tradition of freedom, it now faces the naked problem of rehabilitation, and survival. Her present-day needs are many; her problems in the task of reconstruction are largely the problems of poverty and lack of national resources. These will be overcome. Greece needs help but more than help Greece needs peace and security—peace to build, to think, to work and create a bright new intellectual civilization, one which will continue the tradition.

THE END

INDEX